DESTROY THE PERCEPTIONS

■ ■ ■ ■ ■ ■ ■ ■ ■

Liberate from the Residue of Slavery in a Changing Society

By

Baaki T. Bell

Critical Thoughts Publishing, LLC.
New Jersey

Published in the United States

by

Critical Thoughts Publishing, LLC.
www.criticalthoughtsllc.com
PO Box 3103
Willingboro, NJ 08046

Destroy the Perceptions:
Liberate from the Residue of Slavery in a Changing Society

Baaki T. Bell

Printed in the United States of America

Cover: Design by Royalty Products & Services

ISBN: 978-0-615-79321-4
Library of Congress Control Number: 1911498021

[ii]

Dedication

To Joyce Bell, you are the best Mom anyone can want... Thank you. And in loving memory of Charlie Murphy. Thanks, Grand Daddy... you are not forgotten.

Acknowledgement

To those shoulders I stand on, David Walker, Frederick Douglass, Henry Highland Garnet, W.E.B. Du Bois, Ida B. Wells-Barnett, Jack Johnson, Carter G. Woodson, Marcus Garvey, Paul Robeson, Martin Luther King Jr., Ella Baker, Fannie Lou Hammer, Malcolm X, Muhammad Ali, John Lewis, Amiri Baraka, Jesse Jackson and countless others.

Contents

Baaki Tafiti Bell is Executive Director of the Tafiti Institute for Cultural Awareness and Social Progression

DESTROY THE PERCEPTIONS

■ ■ ■ ■ ■ ■ ■ ■

Liberate from the Residue of Slavery in a Changing Society

INTRODUCTION

THIS SHORT BOOK is by no means a criticism of Black men, as this author is proud and unashamedly Black. In addition, I am a product of the diversity and cultural richness of the Black experience, similar to most Black men throughout this country. Therefore, I embrace the uniqueness and beauty that makes up the Black community in this society. Fervently, promoting its strengths and advocating for improvement in areas requiring growth.

Though brief, this book seeks to stimulate dialogue on how Black men opine about their lives, family and the Black experience. This work is not intended to be an in-depth composition on injustices inflicted against Black people. However, it is impossible to talk about the Black experience without referencing atrocities now or since the inception of "North America's race base slave institution" and its' demise. Moreover, the centuries of oppression and suppression inflicted on what is reported to be the world oldest people. Let alone, the aftermath left on Black America and this society as a whole.

This book's objective is not to expound on the myriad of instances detailing the overt and covert discrimination embedded in society's social discourse. Nor, the structural institutions that limit Black people equality contemporarily. That would require ten volumes, maybe more. This is not a scholarly essay or an attempt at opening up new lines on back to Africa conversations—who holds claim to Egypt (Kemet) — when Black men were Kings, and how impressive they were. As well, how Blacks, must look to the mother continent (Africa) for strength. In the same vein, the extremely optimistic— Black people have to "Unite" argument is not made.

Neither, is this an attack on white people. Nor, is a pass given to visceral racism—the underpinning of this society. Likewise, an in-depth sugarcoating composition on why some Black people self-brutalize is not offered.

Although these topics have significant merit and are important, they are not the focus of this book. Rather, the aim of this exercise is to move forward, by initiating and re-energizing conversations; utilizing five hundred plus years of knowledge, accomplishments, failures, struggles, debates and examination of African descent people existence and experiences in this western hemisphere as reference.

This book's primary focus is on Black men, as this country's social and demographic landscape changes. Thus, a critique on facets of the contemporary African American male experience is rendered to facilitate conversations.

Moreover, a framing of the innumerable perceptions— men of African descent have been linked with since their introduction into this space is provided. Expounding, on how these perceptions remain—shaping the thoughts and behavior of many in society—Black, White, and otherwise. Lastly, the truth regarding Black males in this space defined as the United States is submitted.

In the following chapters, thoughts and suggestions are shared, with hopes of inducing critical thinking to motivate many within Black America to adjust their belief systems.

There is optimism that this book influences those Black men, who consent to the status quo; engage in *Blacknesia*, denial, excuse-rendering and pernicious lifestyles. Moreover, those men who practice internalized racism and the many that live in the then and there, trapped theorizing someone owes them something.

The past cannot be changed. However, the present and future can be directed. This author's humble opinion is the Black man's efforts are best-applied enhancing self, family, and the community, but never forgetting the past. Yet, learning from and building upon it; making positive marks on their space. So, rather than, practicing internalized racial oppression, victimology, remaining silent to injustice and racism, fear of challenging inequality, unawareness, and wavering on impediments of self-progress—Black men must embrace self, redefine objectives, and move progressively forward.

To that end, the scourge of ignorance, and the residual effect of slavery must be tackled to yield peace of mind for future generations. Understanding, liberation of thought enhances the chance to obtain dreams Black ancestors had for their descendants.

CHAPTER ONE
Confusion
■ ■ ■ ■ ■ ■ ■ ■ ■

CLAUDE MCKAY wrote in 1921, *"Although she feeds me bread of bitterness, and sinks into my throat her tiger's tooth, stealing my breath of life, I will confess I love this cultured hell that tests my youth! Her vigor flows like tides into my blood, giving me strength erect against her hate"[1]*

Those words reflect the reality, and perplexing state of life for Black men in this space (North America) during 1921 and contemporarily.

At present, a man of African descent is president of the most powerful country in the world. This historic first has been inspirational, momentous, and progressive. Black men should view this as a clear indicator of the attitudinal, demographic, and political shifts at play in this society.

Black people should enjoy the moment; surely, it represents a step in the right direction. In the process of critical assessment, they must analyze the impact on them and their space, as well. Keeping in mind a significant portion of Black America, chiefly, the inner cities remain impoverished with Black people living in debilitating and dilapidating conditions, driven by unemployment, substandard housing, educational limitations, unawareness, crime and racism.

Thus, consideration has to be given to the question—does having a Black president improve these circumstances. The Black experience, in inner cities has not changed the past fifty years. This is regardless of empirical evidence of growth in Black municipal leadership, income, job titles, post-secondary education and neighborhood relocation (inner city Black flight). Nothing, however, suggests sufficient progress to off-set the poor quality of life for most Blacks who remain in the cities. Expressly, those bound to a zip code in Black population hubs like, Detroit, Camden, Buffalo, Cleveland, Newark, Oakland, Chicago, St. Louis, Memphis, Flint, Baltimore, Compton, D.C., Trenton, Philadelphia, etc.

Therefore, it can be concluded the first term of Black presidential leadership, did not present any notable change to the overall Black experience. Nothing realized so far, besides the "feel good" sensation of another Black first and the warmth of seeing him on MSNBC or CNN. What were Black people expecting? President Obama lives in a political box. The election of President Obama can be seen as symbolism at its finest. So, can and should symbolism be critiqued? Of course, it can and should be.

Nevertheless, the majority of Black people continue to be passionate supporters of President Obama. While it can be argued, President Obama has been effective in enacting a few policies, which will have a universal effect on Americans short and long-term quality of life, in particular, the milestone of his presidency to date—healthcare reform. However, nothing tangible the majority of Black people can hold onto in the midst of economic uncertainty, and the lingering effects of this society's oppressive, suppressive and racial attitudes.

This claim of course prompts Black egalitarians, elitist, and contemporary integrationist to argue President Obama is the president of all the people, and all the people should be his focus. And, he can only do so much, without the discontent of white people. Followed by white conservatives, who imply he is doing too much for Blacks, Latinos, the poor and downtrodden. These are exciting conversations to take up. However, they are conversations for another day. But, ones that surely need to occur.

So, in spite of the absence of any noteworthy developments that focuses on Black people concerns alone, like immigration reform, which will have a tremendous impact on the Hispanic/Latino community. Black people remain hopeful. But hope is not enough when people are hungry, homeless, cold, covertly discriminated against, marginalized and unaware.

How Things Remain the Same

The veteran warriors of the struggle often speak of yesterday's fight for equality. They reference—Martin, Malcolm, the various Movements, the Marches, the Panthers, SNCC, and the NAACP (with teeth), and how things have changed, but remain the same.

Things remaining the same could explain why white police and white citizens, kill Black males and are rarely convicted. Moreover, why, cemeteries are full of young Black males with potential never realized, as more and more become permanent residents at the hotel of death. And, why many young men present to be cohorts of witlessness—exhibiting behavior resembling the newly freed slaves (ignorant), yet, without the determination to learn, enhance self or resist the trappings of unawareness.

So, rather than, the bygone fight songs, "Say it loud—I am Black and proud," or "We shall overcome," as championed in the 1960s and 1970s (now, sung primarily, during the Martin Luther King, Jr., tributes or some other reflective occasion). Many young men, new march songs refer to glorification of a flamboyant lifestyle, pimping, being a gangster—getting paid, laid or both. "What's Going On" needs to be asked again. As the title and lyrics of a song, sung soulfully by Marvin Gaye did.

Equally, young men who do not subscribe to the irrational philosophy of getting paid and laid seem uninformed to the current state of Black America. And the impact societal changes will have on their lives. In the same sand box of confusion are numerous Black males acculturated with a European-American worldview, and a false sense of self as their comfort zone. Especially, since the election and reelection of President Obama serves as an artificial crux.

Yet, what is most alarming in this state of confusion, uncertainty, and *"Blacknesia"* are the many educated and fortunate Black American men engaged in their own construct of internalized racism. Particularly, those Black men in denial (Shhhh... do not talk about that) who separate and shun the Black community for a stake in white America. This group represents a growing segment of the contemporary Black male, expanding the Black experience complexity.

Internalized racial oppression and denial scenarios play out in the Black communities' churches, schools, and elitist organizations as much today as in the 20th century. This continued state of skin tone bias or complexionism, right neighborhood residency, best education premise, and right group—right club elitism still hampers communal synergy.

In the same way, continued unawareness, limited self-assertion and foolish participation in self-exploitation hold many Black men prisoners, dependent on a system resembling a child feeding on its mother's breast.

So regardless of indicators of progression, too many Black men continue to be reliant on elements within society that profits from their ignorance, failures, and denial. It is unfortunate that many Black men still need the Freedmen's Bureau—it has not died. It is very much alive and well. In its current state, it goes by several different names (Social Service Agencies, Government Assistance Programs, Job Training Programs, Welfare, WIC, Food Stamps, EOF, First Family, etc.). Various external and internal factors force reliance on these life-support programs; further, allowing those in the majority population holding racist views to justify and maintain a false sense of superiority.

Regrettably, a significant number of Black men fabricate a false reality—not just affecting them, but their children and the community. Neglecting to control what opportunities or powers, they possess in this society, as they yield to a limited view of self and a distorted worldview.

"The facing of so vast a prejudice could not but bring the inevitable self-questioning, self-disparagement, and lowering of ideals which ever accompany repression and breed in an atmosphere of contempt and hate." **—W.E.B. Du Bois**[2]

[10]

CHAPTER TWO
Setting the Table
■ ■ ■ ■ ■ ■ ■ ■ ■

IN 1926, LANGSTON HUGHES wrote, *"I, too, sing America...Tomorrow, I'll be at the table when company comes. Nobody' will dare say to me, "Eat in the kitchen," then. Besides, they'll see how beautiful I am and be ashamed."*[3]

Over the past decade, there has been an air of excitement in the political realm of the Black experience. It can be reasoned this is because of electing and reelecting America's first Black president. As well, election of the second Black governor, the appointment of the first Black US attorney general, and having two Black US secretaries of state serve back-to-back. For sure, America has seen the greatest top-level movement in its racial political landscape, since reconstruction.

Piggybacking on these phenomena, questions can be proposed and answered. Has progressive steps in the right direction been made the past one hundred years... undoubtedly! Has the lifestyle of many Blacks improved the last four decades, in particular, the emergence of a Black middle-income class... without question! Are more Blacks educated, creating for them a better standard of living than sharecropping or life under the suppression of Jim Crow... of course! Has racism and discrimination subsided? That depends on your point of view. Some claim it has decreased, although slight—with a transformation into different mechanisms of delivery. Others suggest not at all (referencing Trayvon Martin and Stop and Frisk), and there are others, who claim this is now a post-racial society.

Which makes one wonder; does this post-racial banter mean white America has become ashamed of its history of racism, oppression, and dehumanization against Blacks and others? Have they recognized the Black man's strength, contributions to the world stage past and present—also their intelligence? Occurrences during the 2012 Presidential election, Republican primaries, the Trayvon Martin verdict, and other activities suggest racism is alive and well, so that argument is highly questionable.

Nonetheless, progress has occurred in a general sense. Yet, even with progressive steps realized, Black America remains highly challenged, in particular, the Black male.

Black America at its core is unique, diverse and complex (national, regional and local). Black thought and experiences are shaped by culture and circumstance (social-economics, spiritual, and exposure above all). Nevertheless, the continued failure to define itself clearly, and stabilize in this space (United States) over the past one hundred and fifty years enhances the complexity of the Black experience.

Black Americas, complexity makes clear many issues remain unresolved, regardless of obvious social progression. Thus, the wake up alarm has sounded again with changing demographics, politics, and attitudes engulfing this society, specifically, the Latino, Asian and LGBT movements. Yet, most African American men do not appear to be listening or seeing. Some seem to be moving in reverse, while society moves forward. Many more are off-centered culturally (this assumes once being centered or having a degree of Black consciousness). Others have withdrawn into deeper denial. Most Blacks yield to emulation and pseudo assimilation. These developments can be extrapolated are the result of perceived social progression, or a continued state of confusion.

If social progression is the case, some Black men may never benefit from any recent occurrences because their slave residue hinders them. Their unwillingness or inability to grow in intellect, and discover self proves to be quite damaging. On the other hand, perhaps the history of oppression and suppression that still defines the United States of America is too thick to overcome.

And, if confusion is the case, it explains why many within Black communities are now believers in the illusion— identified as a post-racial society. This utopia, where content of character is the benchmark is welcomed, and may come one day, but it is not present today. Nonetheless, some Black men have placed themselves on the hill branded for the Overcame Brother *(college educated, middle-income, Black male in denial)*. They appear to think and behave as if a post-racial society currently exists.

> *"The large majority of the Negroes who have put on the finishing touches of our best colleges are all but worthless in the development of their people."* —**Carter G Woodson**[4]

Shifting Society

Barack H. Obama II, the 44th President of the United States, has been elected twice because of the changing demographics of this society and political shifts in opinions. Yet sorry to say, most white Americans did not vote for him. President Obama, won reelection with only 39% of the white vote overall.[5] Those in the majority population appear not to possess a fondness for the societal shifts. However, the train has left the station, and cannot be stopped. But, try they must and will.

The 2012, election reaffirms America is a polarized society. Opening up further discussion that white America is concerned with the loss of privilege and overall power to shape policy (see the Republican Party scramble). Does this sound familiar (reconstruction and southern whites quest to redeem the south, and northern whites aim to control and suppress Blacks)?

As the new political and societal shifts unfold, where do Black American men stand in this contemporary amalgamation? Where do they stand in a society, comfortable with using racial coding in politics and the media; moreover, practicing overt and covert racism to maintain the status quo?

Equally, how do Black men view an evolving diverse social, political, and economic dispersed Black community— redefining what once was considered Black, Blackness, Black consciousness, and the Black experience?

It is safe to say that the majority population does not embrace Black people fully, in spite of all the contributions made to this country. But, also do not express overt disdain, as much as in the past. Of course, this is a matter of opinion. Yet, still, where do Black men stand reliving the same issues decade after decade (poverty, housing, limited education, unemployment, crime and internalized racism)?

Now that a man of African ancestry has been elected president for the second time... have Blacks overcome? Are they still waiting for equality, a resurgence of white abolitionist guilt or the big transformation to post-racialism?

Not being able to answer these questions in a congruent voice magnifies the Black man's position in this American project. It is obvious many Black men have moved away from the principles of Black affirmation, self-determination, and self-sustainment advocated during post reconstruction, the early 20th century, the 1950s, 1960s and 1970s. Thus, self-identification or "Black consciousness" gains realized during the Civil Rights and Black Power Movements appear to have retracted.

Blacks fight no more

The transformation actions the past fifty years have resulted in advances without question (educational opportunities, military service advancement, income, homeownership, and political positions). Yet the cost appears to be repression of Black self-identify, self-concept, and self-assertiveness—resulting in an intense emulation of the white dominant culture. In contrast, other cultures—Asian and Hispanic/Latino appear to maintain strong cultural identity as they integrate into America's fabric. Slavery forced cultural suppression, and contemporary fears of being considered anti-social, anti-white, and anti-American, drive many Blacks to straddle a supposed necessary fence.

Self-empowerment championed by those who struggled to define a Black experience in a most hostile environment from Frederick Douglass, Martin Delany, and Alexander Crummell—up to—Booker T. Washington, W.E.B. Du Bois, Marcus Garvey, A. Phillip Randolph, Martin Luther King, Jr., Elijah Muhammad, Malcolm X, Stokely Carmichael, Amiri Baraka and many others seems no more.

From the current state of the Black experience, it can be reasoned defining a Black-self is no longer highly sought, nor valued, some suggest not even necessary.

Black self-empowerment and assertiveness appears to go against the contemporary Black integrationist, egalitarian, post-racial, and *Overcame Brother* models.

These models seem naïve... in the wake of society's perceived racial progression, while some Black men have achieved, far too many have not... why? Perhaps the continued weight of suppression is the answer. Conversely, lack of achievement may be the result of unawareness, questionable educational pursuits, limited civil engagement, as well as a failure to self-assert, which can be cogently argued has a direct relationship to suppression.

Not asserting implies acceptance of the status quo (inferior state-in-inferior space, massed by pseudo equality). Furthermore, as implied, the weight of suppression may be too heavy to lift as new covert (stealth) forms of containment are being implemented in desperation. Moreover, it hints that a pardoning of white America for its atrocities, racism and dehumanizing acts against black people has occurred.

Does time heal psychological and physiological wounds; is this form of forgiveness divine? Maybe forgiving and forgetting is necessary to achieve post-racial status. This seems to be the thinking of many Black spiritual leaders trained on Eu-

[17]

rocentric religious concepts and ideology.

Based upon these open questions and numerous other issues, it can be easily surmised being Black remains loathed. This holds true not just in white eyes, but some Blacks as well. Even defining Black has become difficult—unless you watch CNN!

An eradication of "I'm Black, and I'm Proud," has most definitely occurred. Now espoused is—I am not Black; I am mixed, bi-racial, multiracial, part-Native American, Creole, French, Puerto Rican, Dominican, or universal!...Why can't I just be an American? Many Black people have adopted an avid aversion too identification as an accomplished person, who is unashamedly Black. What has manifested as the new Black champion appears to be a no self-concept, not in touch with reality lack of culture person in denial. This suggests widespread ambiguity throughout Black communities exist, and lack of self-identification remains at the emergence of a shifting society.

Unfortunately, this ambiguity includes those Black men who live in a strange state of retrogression, or a paradigm shift backwards. This uncertainty negates seeing that the face of America is rapidly changing. America once dominated by white Anglo-Saxon Protestants fixation with ethnocentrism, xenophobia and racism—is being transformed. Not since the heyday of Ellis Island, has America seen such a face-lift.

[18]

While this occurs, most Blacks continue to advocate, adopt and practice Eurocentric-American concepts. All the while, white America struggles to hold firm too yesterday, seeking to maintain power and control. It is apparent; those in power clearly do not have an identity issue.

And as this societal face-lift ensues, some argue Black America's one hundred and fifty year journey of unfulfilled self-identification remains a form of self-hate, failed assimilation or realized inferiority. While others contend, change is obvious, regardless that some Blacks do not seem to be growing or achieving. Further, implying this contemporary Black experience is not your father's or grandfather's. Declaring a modern-day Black situation exists where issues prominent in the 1960s, 1970s, 1980s and even the 1990s are outdated, irrelevant, or resolved. Perhaps, some truth exists in this thinking.

On the other hand, it can be reasoned the uninformed, misguided, and disconnected have taken the mantel and elevated to leadership. Forgetting or never knowing whose shoulders they stand on. More importantly, the gains Black people have achieved did not occur without struggle and much resistance from the white majority population. Furthermore, that the struggle continues. If this is a hundred meter dash, maybe, society just crossed the 40-meter mark.

The cost of freedom or justice is never too high. However, some could, and do argue many Blacks contemporarily are conceding much for a title, a contract, a department head, a news desk position or talk show, as well as a federal, state or county job (what choice do they have). Similar to Black ancestry for a plate of food, a blanket, a job in the big house, or a sparing of the lash (yet, those were different times and circumstances). The need to concede implies that racism and discrimination are always present in the room. Perhaps, Blacks conceding is mandated to exist, and achieve in the not realized post-racial society.

Therefore, the question remains, has the educated and non-formularized educated Black man, who has obtained middle or upper-middle income status, immersed himself so far into European-American propaganda and acculturation. So far, that he willfully ignores the realization that a significant portion of Black people in this society are still disenfranchised; struggling in a society never meant to include them, except in a subordinate role.

This question stands unanswered, but regardless of the position one takes—a disconnection from reality is apparent—especially among the *Overcame Brothers*—the champions of the alleged post-racial society. The disconnect is more pronounced with this group of Black men, than those in the inner city who face a truer reality every day.

*"If the "highly educated" Negro would forget most of the untried theories taught him in school, if he could see through the propaganda which has been instilled into his mind under the pretext of education, if he would fall in love with his own people and begin to sacrifice for their uplift—if the "highly educated" Negro would do these things, he could solve some of the problems now confronting the race"—***Carter G. Woodson**[6]

Slave Residue Remains

Even though a Black man occupies the White House, continued abasement to the white dominant populace historical design is obvious. Acquiescing to characterizations that Black men are belligerent, churlish, possess limited intelligence, low achievers, and problematic with a few exceptions remain intact—more profound, or subtle depending on one's space.

One can sense the stench of slavery remains on the body, causing denseness within the mind of many Black men. It is conceived residue remains because they have not developed a sustainable construct in this space. Moreover, they are unsure of their place in this changing landscape. And have been uncertain of their role in this caste, class, and color society since the end of the civil rights and Black power movements. The changing landscape visible to the eye, reaffirms the concept of Blackness is dissipating or being redesigned.

Black people, as it stand are unable to maintain dominion over their alleged space. This is apparent by taking heed to shifts in power and population in once majority Black cities and towns.

Albeit, population shifts taking place, it is important to possess an appreciation for different cultures. Societal interfacing is germane to growth. Thus, valuing the multitude of cultures that now populate American society—dictates future movement. However, knowledge begins with self. Currently, many in the Black masses demonstrate a disoriented concept of self.

What is most disturbing is the disoriented concept of self, highlights failure to obtain, or acknowledge the necessity for psychological healing after hundreds of years of programing (internalized racism and the disproportionate number of Black-on-Black killing speaks for itself). Many prominent Black therapists and scholars have referenced this point, in particular, Dr. Na'im Akbar.[7] Introspection of the home, community, and lifestyle choices suggests many Black men need deprogramming and psychological rehabilitation. This has been the case since 1865.

Most recent, Dr. Joy Degruy Leary suggested the scarring of Black people could be identified as posttraumatic slave syndrome.[8] This may be true....The conditioning appears unyielding after centuries of reinforcement. Unfortunately, many Black men are oblivious to its existence.

Their reality is equated to the inhabitants in the popular movie the *Matrix* (Warner Brothers Pictures, 1999). As in the movie, most residents are not aware; they are captives in a comatose state. One can say that a significant number of Black men took the *blue pill.*

"Psychological freedom, a firm sense of self-esteem, is the most powerful weapon against the long night of physical slavery."
— **Martin Luther King, Jr.**[9]

Even though this psychological imprisonment prevails, history tells the story of those champions, who freed themselves from mental shackles, fought against oppression and suppression, and achieved immense success in the past. Current data, plus personal witness reveals those who continue to excel in this still turbulent, but encouragingly complex environment called America (*governors, mayors, business leaders, scientist, athletes, etc.).* Their accomplishments are worthy of emulation, too numerous to mention, and too great not to recognize.

Black people possess extraordinary talent and resiliency, having achieved remarkable things in a society where their fate has always been predisposed. Many notable personalities from the past understood, and today's current inspirations understand the relevancy of their second sight as inferred by W.E.B. Du Bois.[10]

Yet, in spite of success by those paving the way, there are Black American men who demonstrate thinking and behavior ruinous to communal well-being, as well as themselves....Why? Confused people (one man's confusion is another man's logic, if he does not understand his conditioning), plague many communities. It definitely is not limited to the Black experience. Except action that undermines growth in Black communities, is cancerous because of the history of deprivation. This age-old issue is a constant *hanging Chad*; a variable several in the majority population utilize to justify distorted views.

Whom to blame

Ignorance and poverty are crippling constructs in Black America, the foundation created by some European-American ancestors. And, contemporarily some seem to desire to maintain them. These constructs provide those in white America that adhere to racism and discrimination a blanket of deniability. Many argue these constructs were gleaned from America's oppression and suppression of Black ancestors. If accurate, it can be deduced these constructs are the starting point for inappropriate exploits and internalized racial oppression. However, this correlation... let alone causation is seldom given its due credit by the majority population.

Moreover, Black men no longer challenge those who constructed this absurdity with committed zeal. Satisfaction with progression during the last fifty years may be the reason. Many Blacks do not want to rock the boat, or put their state or federal job in jeopardy. Nor do Black men confront with similar commitment segments of the Black populace that engage in nefarious acts, or exhibit baseless ideology; practice *"Black-nesia,"* or victimology. Thus, unity may never be achieved, which some speculate is the answer to the contemporary *"Black Problem."*

Along the same lines, Black people do not challenge local political leaders on crime and poverty plaguing the community. They do not challenge school superintendents and school boards on predominantly Black schools academic under performance. Let alone attend a PTA meeting (parents... where are you?). Black children are not competing. Many reports suggest they do not perform well on standardized examinations compared with white children. This includes Black youth, who live in middle and upper-middle class settings.

Which factors contribute to this underachievement contemporarily? Whose fault is this—Black people in predominate-black communities today run many school districts? What role do parents, in particular, fathers play in their child's academic success or failure? Can Blacks continue to argue inadequate resources is the reason Black children are not competing? Are Black teachers and administrators capable of using educational models normed and standardized on systems that do not consider the Black experience?[11]

Whatever the model, clearly a lack of education serves as a gateway to a life of poverty, frustration and for a significant number of Black men—a relationship with criminality. Secure government jobs at the post office, county agencies, or auto plants are a rarity today.

And because of limited education, employment opportunities, racism, and lack of awareness—prisons and jails overflow with Black males mentally immature, as well as ill-equipped to engage society in a constructive way. They are trapped in a modern convict leasing system, where profits motivate prison developers and operators.

The effect of crime on them [Black men] and society has been explored at length. W.E.B. Du Bois examined this phenomenon in the *Philadelphia Negro* (1899). Recently, Michelle Alexander in *The New Jim Crow* (2010) and Khalil Gibran Muhammad in *The Condemnation of Blackness* (2011) wrote about this troubling issue, which has magnified since the beginning of the 20th century. The business of Black male incarnation is a multimillion-dollar industry.

In stark contrast, it appears a significant number of Black men are shareholders at the prison industrial complex, striving to keep their investment viable by their constant re-entry. Never learning from past mistakes or failing to change directions (this is very difficult once that initial mistake is made). Their ignorance and societal requirements (check the box) make them frequent guest at the steel bar and barbwire hotel. Recidivism, while disturbingly high in Black communities—

remains generally unquestioned by Black people.

What do the changing dynamics of society (technology, population shifts, reduction in manual labor) have in store for these men upon returning to the community?

For the most part, Black men are products of their social-ization, like everyone else; many born into a cultural construct engulfed in belief systems knee-deep in unawareness, poverty, etc. (by grand design, perhaps). This is accompanied by an embedded contemptuous view of self, constant doubt and a need for self-centered gains. Many Blacks possess an innate desire to prove themselves acceptable to the white majority populace. White societal respect, acknowledgement, and ap-proval are compelling forces for Black people.

The need to prove to white America, relevancy has been engrained in Black Americans psyche since emancipation. The need to engage in a societal paradigm that in many ways devalues Blacks participation and marginalizes their contribu-tions in general, remains in-bedded. This social construct is clearly recognizable, unless one subscribes to the current post-racial theory being espoused by various academics, so-called political experts on talk shows and of course by the Overcame Brothers.

So, as a part of this societal construct, many within the Black experience remain comatose. Not only do they not see the changing landscape, but also the limited positive Black male leadership in the community, the few Black male professionals and lack of Black male stewardship in the home. In addition, they do not seem to fully comprehend their role in this over five hundred-year stage play.

More specifically, certain Black men appear to accept the regalia of complacency or worse develop practices to do less, have less and expect nothing. What happen to the zest after 1865, during World War I, the Harlem Renaissance, Chicago Renaissance, and the 1950s, 1960s and 1970s? Maybe the improvements realized over the past few years nullified the thirst for equality, growth and success for some. Then again, perhaps, the current state of affairs (first Black president, Black governor, etc.) has satisfied others hunger, so they are full.

Is the construct, the majority populace promotes regarding Black males valid? Definitely not, yet, one could contend that some Black men are stewards of obscure thinking. They are unmoved, nor stunned by the news shows, newspapers and internet propaganda reporting the shortcoming and negative exploits of their fellow Black male.

Without question, certain Black men are desensitized regarding various community issues. Observation of Black communities in despair supports this. Even if, the root of these issues are the fault of the majority's population treatment and policies, as many claim and an enormous body of evidence

[28]

supports—the facts are a vast number of Black families live within the space called cities, where a number of issues take place. So black people have to own it, control it and make it work.

Call to action

With all these issues in Black communities, where is the outrage? Where is the determination to change, challenge, and uplift? Have Blacks loss their will to fight, or would that be considered by contemporary standards, too radical, anti-American, anti-social behavior or anti-white? Where is the disappointment and disgust of data that approximates one million Black males are incarcerated around the country? This constitutes roughly 40% of the nation's total prison population.[12] Black Americans, as a whole makes up slightly above 2.9% of the national body, reported in the latest U.S. Census.[13]

Where is the comprehensive questioning of illogical numbers of Black male incarceration, and the attack on crime, illiteracy, poverty and such? Where and who are those responsible? Where is the community assessment and call to action on others, as well as itself?

Has the real Black voice been muted, or become so whitewashed it has no bite? Is the Black voice now lead by Black Ivy League graduates, imbued with Eurocentric thought, who migrate to predominate Black communities, which they have no real loyalty, but their self-centered motives drives them to placate the community and promote themselves?

Since, most of the typical responses no longer can articulate the impediments encapsulating the Black experience. Hence, questions require answering—are Black men dumb, and childlike. The former oppressors often suggested they were in the past. And, some in the majority still insinuate; except, when referring to the perceived exceptions, such as, President Barack Obama, Eric Holder, Deval Patrick, Cory Booker, Kasim Reed (mayor of Atlanta), or Kenneth Frazier (chairman, CEO of Merck).

Moreover, are African American men mentally and physically different, which hinder their abilities to excel, as concluded by many yesterday (including Thomas Jefferson) and today? Do Black men still need the descendants of their former oppressors and others, who advocated for departure back to Africa, the Caribbean or Latin America to hold them up? Better yet, do they still need the descendants of those who bombed, spit, burnt, and lynched Blacks to provide for and feed them?

Conversely, are Black men asleep and bemused; did they abdicate their position as the paternal line to the world civilizations, did their wayward children rebel and take the kingdom?

Perhaps the continued emasculation of the Black man's manhood is the problem. Has regular defaming of their humanity left them beaten down and unwilling to fight back, challenge or critique what seems to be an indefensible and unbeatable opponent? Why is there just a scant few Black men standing up and fighting the good fight today, compared with the past?

In contrast, has the lure of corporate employment, federal and state employment, a job title, membership at the golf club, and a different neighborhood made things all better, thereby, supporting—forgetting and forgiving? Is it better to join them, than fight them? Do Blacks see their own role in the community trials?

Frederick Douglas, W.E.B. Du Bois, E. Franklin Frazier, James Farmer, Martin Luther King, Jr., and many more advocated for integration or pseudo assimilation—is this still the way? Is copying every step of the descendants of the former slave masters, and others who transgressed against African Americans ancestry the lifeline to growth? Again, do Blacks possess any other real choices? Does embracing the status quo ensure—life, liberty and the pursuit of happiness? It has not thus far for many. Maybe it will—in the post-racial world. Perhaps, the adoption of a multicultural lens to meet a changing society is the key.

"A man who stands for nothing will fall for anything."
-Malcolm X [14]

CHAPTER THREE
Progress means not making an Excuse
■ ■ ■ ■ ■ ■ ■ ■ ■

A WORD TO THE BLACK MAN
DO NOT POINT YOUR NOSE TOO HIGH
DO NOT SWELL YOUR CHEST TOO MUCH
DO NOT BOAST TOO LOUDLY
DO NOT BE PUFFED UP
LET NOT YOUR AMBITION BE INORDINATE
OR TAKE A WRONG DIRECTION
REMEMBER YOU HAVE DONE NOTHING AT ALL
YOU ARE JUST THE SAME MEMBER OF SOCIETY YOU WERE LAST WEEK
YOU ARE ON NO HIGHER PLANE
DESERVE NO NEW CONSIDERATION
AND WILL GET NONE
NO MAN WILL THINK A BIT HIGHER OF YOU
BECAUSE YOUR COMPLEXION IS THE SAME
OF THAT OF THE VICTOR AT RENO

--LOS ANGELES TIMES JULY 5, 1910

WHAT A MOMENT IN TIME. One can only imagine when Jack Johnson became the heavyweight champion of the world, how Black people felt. It disrupted the white supremacy narrative for sure. It is postulated it filled Black men with a sense of pride never experienced, especially, the former slaves. Jack Johnson was a man. He lived life as a free man, without making excuses.

Nearly a hundred years later *another moment to remem-*

ber: Many said it aloud, others thought it, but never said it, but most African descendant people felt it, a sense of pride and joy never experienced. Millions of African Americans cried and shouted in jubilation—*We did it....We did it! I would have never believed it... not in my lifetime. Man,...We got a Black president. We made it to the mountaintop! The struggle is no more. Barack is going to change the country's view of the Black man!*

The Black President

The presidential victory of 2008 overwhelmed many with a sense of pride and instilled a feeling of redemption swelling hearts with euphoria. The inauguration of the first Black President of the United States was quite memorable to say the least. To witness the President and the First Lady stroll down Pennsylvania Avenue seemed like something out of a fairy tale movie. It was an incredible picture. Watching the President and First Lady dance at the inaugural balls caused warmth in the body, which lasted for weeks. The world was witnessing Black love at its finest. The President with his family put the beauty of the Black family on display. Not since the *Cosby Show* had America seen such a positive Black family image on the national stage. However, this was reality, not a sitcom.

The meanness of the streets, blight within the community, unemployment, the country at war, economic uncertainty, and the depth of despair for a moment... for just a moment... seemed to stand still, as the world watched in enjoyment while history was realized.

The Sequel: The script could not have been written better. President Barack Obama reelected in 2012. The inauguration, his speech, the parade, and inaugural balls displayed a man full of confidence. The First Lady and first family looked lovelier than ever.

Yet hold up! Before ordering a Mercedes, and putting a chicken in everyone's pot, let us pump the brakes and stop the presses... reality check! Black folks do not want to make the same mistake of expecting too much again. It has been four plus years since that first moment, and several more years to be had. The hope is that President Obama's second term, will offer more tangible results Black people can see and touch... minus the feel good emotions.

The President during his second term may alter the makeup of the Supreme Court, advancing the demographic landscape and attitude shift. How will that affect Black people? Only time will tell. He, also, may have an opportunity to enact policy, which stimulates employment (roads, bridges, and other infrastructure). Currently, Black unemployment remains the highest of any group in the country. Many Black children are struggling, living in poverty and crime-festered neighborhoods. This has been the case before he took office and remains so, as stated earlier. Fathers are missing in action from the household (this has been the case since slavery) and the list goes on.

Were Blacks' expectations too high the first term? Many believed they were. Should Blacks expectations of President Obama different from other presidents who have sat in the chair? Black people face serious issues daily, more than most.

But to gain a deeper understanding of this presidency, and keep things in perspective, all must realize President Obama exists in a political box. Moreover, he has, and will continue to deal with a litany of issues and challenges as the first black president. He is the first Black president of a nation built upon theft from indigenous people, enslavement, racism, oppression and suppression of others. And as President, he and the world has been reminded of how Black men are viewed and treated in the United States by segments within the majority population.

To expound, some in society have shown a lack of respect for the first Black president. Unlike any time in this country's history of presidential leadership, has a president been so attacked. Many neoconservatives have displayed a deliberate distain for President Obama.

Why did this occur during his first term (yes, this simply answered question is asked)? Indeed, he is one of the smartest men ever to sit in the chair. He has shown leadership, calm and integrity during a trying time. And he has achieved. The effects of his achievements remain debatable—but he has achieved, without question. He seems to have the majority of the people's interest at heart. Could it be because a distinctive part of society cannot accept a man of African heritage sitting in the highest office in this land? Does *visceral hatred* run that deep?

The presidential election candor of 2012, states it does. Furthermore, recent polls claim a majority of white people still possess an anti-Black view.[15]

During the pathway to reelection of President Obama, the rhetoric from the President's non-supporters attempted to re-define him and his presidency. Frequently, conservatives, tea party members and Republican leadership tried to depict the president as a governmental aid who made horrendous errors. Consistently, using disrespectful attacks to frame him, such as—You Lie! I dare you call yourself Mr. President. You are not even a citizen. I will wave my finger in your face. Your thinking is foreign, un-American. These were just a few of the attacks on President Obama's Americanism.

History tells us American born Africans were once con-sidered foreigners. This was one of the justifications for en-slavement (Dred Scott case, 1857). The United States Su-preme Court supported this position at one point, led by Chief Justice Roger Taney and his views of Black people *"So far*

[36]

inferior that they had no rights which the white man was bound to respect."[16]

As much as Black people appreciate seeing President Obama in the White House. They empathize with the tough job he inherited to stabilize and grow the country's economy. Moreover, Black men sense the pain every time he is disrespected and berated—as most Black men can relate to this in some form or fashion.

In spite of defaming tactics by the Republican candidate(s), the people spoke—reelecting President Obama. The reelection resounded loudly, suggesting to the Republican Party to reassess their platform. But, it appears they have yet to heed the warning. Change is rapidly occurring in terms of population dynamics and attitudes in many homes... so say the polls.

Yet still, the blatant insolence toward the first black president, the deaths of Sean Bell, Oscar Grant III, and Trayvon Martin, as well as numerous other unnamed victims of racism, puts forth the question—what is the Black man's worth in this society today? His previous value is well known. Does presidential election racism and death at the hands of white men answer the question, and serve as a continued reminder of the Black male supposed place?

Clear, distinct ideological differences exist between Black and white people. And because of these philosophical differences, most whites and blacks see the American experience uniquely opposite. One sees it full of opportunity, the other full of restrictions, impediments, and suppression.

Despite, positive gains the past few decades—beginning with the civil rights and voting rights acts, enhanced post-secondary education, increased income and the electing and reelecting a man of African descent president of the United States. Most Blacks, however, would say not enough has been accomplished, as America continues to be a society where the stench of slavery, oppression and suppression persist.

Time to Regroup

The contemporary misfortunes of Black America are amplified by acts of self-brutalization and mental captivity. This is spearheaded by the countless deaths of Black males at the hands of Black males (Chicago, Detroit, Camden, Memphis, St. Louis, etc.). These acts speak louder to some than the Martin and Bell deaths, or the attempted defaming of President Obama. Acts of violence against fellow Blacks equate to the mass murdering, and other ignorant vicious deeds committed against Blacks after the civil war, during reconstruction, and the early 20th century by racist southern and northern whites, maybe even worst.

Black on Black acts of terrorism holds the community hostage. Along with, unemployment, fatherless homes, limited education achievement, poverty, and recidivism—serve as clear indicators why Black men must regroup and reassess themselves in this contemporary environment.

The objective should remain to aid the community that birthed them, and they have a stake in. But, another progressive chapter of the Black experience is compelled, which includes enhanced engagement in the social, economic and political discourse with a focus on *stability* and *sustainability*. The shifting demographics and Blacks current positions necessitate cognitive reframing to grasp the subtleties of the new societal milieu.

Blacks contributions to the country's growth and development before and since its inception are undeniable, but often are. The blood, sweat and tears of Blacks assisted in shaping America's general culture, as well as building its infrastructure. Thus, they cannot separate from it... nor can it separate from them. Black people are forever a part of the social fabricate of this society.

Thus, a sense of Black pride and self-assertiveness is called upon again. No longer can Black men afford the position of victim, as some appear comfortable with it. Instead, contemporary solutions to achieve victory in all facets are called for—welcoming support, suggestions, and constructive criticism from others who have a stake in Black wellness.

There can be no rest because a man of African descent is

president. Yes, be motivated by the moment. But the small victories to date, although they feel good, only dull the truth for a moment—that most Black communities are in flux. *Some inner cities resemble towns time forgot.*

A uniqueness of Black people in America is demonstrated by their cultural strength. A steel weave exist, which constitutes Black people as one. On various issues, the need to demonstrate oneness in a society that champion's individuality is required. This was the call in the self-help era, the fight against lynching, the Montgomery bus boycott (the straw that stirred the civil rights movement), and the call to *close ranks* during the election and reelection of President Barack Obama. This must be the continued call—for education, poverty elimination and other detriments for greater progress.

No More Excuses

Without question, these remain turbulent waters, but *hopeful times*. Thus, to achieve an enhanced paradigm, there must be an immediate ceasing of excuses and blaming others for the Black man's conundrum.

Challenges to injustice, inequality, and racism of course should and must always occur. However, making excuses and blaming others when it relates to issues outside the box of fair play, a fair playing field, equal opportunity and justice— should not occur. The landscape laid the past one hundred and fifty years is well known. If one lacks knowledge, it is unacceptable. Black men hold the key to their fate, whether they know or accept it....Insomuch, only they can change or modify their current existence.

Yeah, it was said... stop making excuses and blaming others. Several years ago, President Obama received pushback for suggesting Black men (fathers) need to become more responsible. Bill Cosby was attacked verbally in the press for what some viewed as being insensitive to socioeconomically challenged Black people. Mr. Cosby, spoke out about the supposed misuse of resources, instead of perfecting the capacity to read well. He was labeled out of touch with the Black community.

Whether one agrees or not with Mr. Cosby or President Obama's critiques, or the position of those who challenge their assertions; one walks away with a deeper understanding that the Black community is diverse and does not possess a monolithic view.

Although Blacks seldom publicly speak about internal acts or what is perceived as excuses or self-induced hindrances to progress—many whites, rationalize Blacks render excuses for almost everything. Common references to the system; my father was not around; my mother was a single parent in a tough neighborhood; my grandmother raised me; racism held me back, or the white man still got his foot on my neck, are just a few highlighted. While there is no question regarding the validity in these arguments, as they are real life scenes in the Black man's screenplay.

However, they are currently, ineffective, unless you are speaking to some guilt-ridden white woman fresh from getting her license as a social worker. Those responses are put forth to judges, prosecutors, employers, wives, girlfriends and even children. Now the common reply is... yeah, yeah, yeah heard it before, and so has everyone else.

Societal ignorance must be recognized, but not allowed to impede and become an excuse. Immediate movement to the here and now, without forgetting the past, and the shoulders one stands on is necessitated.

More candidly, an in-depth conversation on known variables contributing to chaos in Black communities is demanded. Correlation and causality—should be deliberated as well. Thereafter, solutions based on modifying, adjusting and enhancing aspects of Black cultural ideology must be garnered. As the streets say, *"You already know what it is."*

___

"A little less complaint and whining, and a little more dogged work and manly striving, would do us more credit than a thousand civil rights bills"– **W. E. B. Du Bois**[17]

CHAPTER FOUR
The Conversations
■ ■ ■ ■ ■ ■ ■ ■ ■

SCHOLARS, POLITICIANS, SPIRITUAL LEADERS and LAYMAN argue conversations regarding relevant issues may lead to discovery and solutions. However, today, conversation in the Black community is limited.

So, if Black men are to regroup, rebuild and redirect— honest conversations must be engaged or reengaged on serious issues. Certain issues may make some people uncomfortable.

One issue of importance that requires dialogue is the invisible list of so-called taboos impeding Blacks ability to converse internally. The origin of these prohibited topics is unknown. They seem to be instilled in Blacks during their earliest childhood development. A crazy list of things Black folk should not do or talk about. Some appear to be carryovers from the slave experience and Jim Crow area. Perhaps grandparents, preachers, elders or griots created them, but never wrote them down, so they are recognized as the unwritten don'ts.

Don't Don't...Do It

Mothers and fathers used to express these directives all the time. Such as, don't be in a store with your hands in your pocket, someone might think you stole something. Don't talk about the family business with anybody outside the family. Don't make any sudden moves when stopped by the police. Also, don't talk about Cousin Joe; he is somewhat slow (mentally impaired). And the old favorite—don't talk with too much confidence, you might be thought of as uppity. These directives are still spoken, depending on what area of the country a Black person resides.

Yet the most sacred of the unwritten plants its stakes around internalized racism. Internalized racial oppression remains a cultural tradition—in particular, the championing of light skin and European features over dark skin and African features. Blacks cannot resolve this chasm. Once executed by the master, the color line remains in full effect within the Black community.

In spite of Blacks making headway in all facets of society, the divide created on the plantation continues to cause unrest in the 21st century. The mindset of light skin superiority that permeated on the plantation for hundreds of years is alive and well, and complexionism remains the most recognized form of Black internalized separation.

The Black community appears to be in a time warp, regarding this issue. The late renowned author and activist James Weldon Johnson asserted light-skinned is *"economically necessary,"* and having dark skin is an inconvenience, in one of his most acclaimed works.[18]

Sprung from the proficient psychological and physiological cruelties inflicted on Black women and men by the slave master, Blacks continue to subjugate themselves to variations of this divisive game. Because of the master's conditioning and cultural norming, Blacks fail to engage in dialogue about an issue that results in mental and physical scarring. Therefore, behavior and thinking modeled by adults and children alike passed down through generations persist. Reinforcing the devaluation of dark skin and endorsing the concept that skin and features of Europeans are ideal. Blacks have been programmed to be satisfied with if you are light—all right. If you are dark, do not bark.

This promotes Blacks, not to discuss the effects of sexual relationships between the former oppressors and transgressors of their ancestors. Whether, it was rape, or without force, many light-skinned Blacks, highlight the afterbirth of the act. Glorification of features from raping and breeding— portraying them as traits of betterment causing what seems to be a non-repairable dent in the Black armor. Thus, promoting an unhealthy view of Black beauty, whereby, Blacks frown on African's natural appearance.

Regrettably, this issue is guilty of instituting internalized warfare, triggering some Black girls and boys to loathe their natural appearance. Demonstrating that complexion endures as an ardent divide affecting Black children's self-concept and self-esteem.

Not only do young Black children wrestle with images they see on television, the internet and print, but almost all other forms of societal norming claim Black children need to appear more like white people. They deal day-to-day with fellow Blacks who opine looking like the majority white culture is necessary. Proposing they are not attractive because they are too dark or have African features, so they become the brunt of jokes and often ridiculed. Just ask 2012 Olympic Gold medalist Gabby Douglas how she felt after people commented about her hair and nose.

Nothing is new about this conditioned dogma; it remains an effective means of control. It speaks to destroying Blacks' self-identity throughout the African Diaspora.

Although the topic of light over dark skin has been brought up before, and is well documented, what is perplexing is the inability for Blacks to cure this divide. Many Blacks seem not to want to confront this matter and liberate from the light is right schema. The mindset and behavior maintains a caste and class system within Black communities.

Without question, many Black ancestors intertwined with the majority populace ancestors, shaping physical features and appearance Blacks are conditioned to crave. These unions created mulattoes and every other degree of color-coding. Most of these acts, as stated were brutal sexual exploitation.[19]

"The rape which your gentlemen have done against helpless black women in defiance of your own laws is written on the foreheads of two millions of mulattoes and written in ineffaceable blood" —
W.E.B. Du Bois[20]

Yesterday cannot be changed. An undoing of the raping of thousands—upon thousands of Black women by white males during bondage cannot occur. Moreover, attacks after enslavement of the Black women are also irreversible.[21] However, with all the atrocities inflicted on Black people by others—Blacks can control their actions toward one another.

"The ruffianly element of Southern society, who think that black men have no rights which white men should regard, and black women no virtue which white men should respect"
—Alexander Crummell[22]

As many light-skinned Blacks sought to differentiate from Blacks who happened to be poorer, less educated and darker-complexion in the past. It appears...this practice still exist[23] (social organizations, churches, etc.). Exalting the former captor's blood running through one's veins—shouts to the failure to be free of the slave residue.

The Black community is all too familiar with light-skinned men appealing to the most attractive Black women, dark and light-skinned. Likewise, many dark-skinned Black men sought and seek the light-skinned female, as she is perceived to be more desirable than the dark-skinned Black woman.

Then, there are light-skinned Black people who will only date and marry other light-skinned Blacks, or dark-skinned Black women desiring to share a child with a light-skinned male. What a throwback mindset (get out of the master's house). One effect of these unions is doting over the light-skinned child, praising their supposed attractive features, while in the same instance, finding fault in the dark-skinned child's appearance. Now with the acceptance of inter-racial dating and marriages, we see even more promoting of the so-call attractiveness of biracialism. This form of thinking is counter-productive and a testimonial to confusion and lack of racial appearance pride.

If Blacks live in a post-racial society as many *Overcame Brothers*, and those in white America claim, light skin is *no longer* a necessity for economic stability. Yet if, it does remain an *economic necessity*, it reaffirms the racist climate people of African descent are forced to live in. Moreover, it validates the existence and practice of internalized racism.

Skin, Hair, Eyes, Lips and Noise

All praise to Madame C J. Walker and Garrett A. Morgan. It is easy to see why marketers and advertisers devote significant resources on Black women. Black women spend millions of dollars a year on perms for relaxed hair and bagged hair.

Society has convinced the Black woman, she is not beautiful unless her appearance resembles her white counterpart. As a result, Blacks idolize straight, curly, wavy hair and narrow noses similar to the majority populace in this society. The Black woman alters her appearance to be socially acceptable. Being Black, jet-Black, or purple-Black, possessing tightly curled hair is at direct odds with light skin, wavy or loosely curled hair. This confused view appears to state light is right, as many Blacks yearn to possess hazel, light brown, or green eyes to look more like their former captors—without knowledge of why.

Ignorantly, many Black people joke about this serious matter in the living room, around the kitchen table, and make fun of it in school. In the same sense, they watch absurd TV programs featuring actors, who happen to be light-skinned, with long fake hair and contacts. The laughter, displays the deep-rooted brainwashing, and supports the need for rethinking and conversation.

Meanwhile, the beauty supply owners (Korean marketers, in particular) cachinnate all the way to the bank. Store bought artificial hair, fade cream; light skin and colored contact lenses are prerequisite for the movies, the music videos, the television industry and acceptance in mainstream America. This seems like a throwback to the Cotton Club, 1930s, 1940s, 1950s, and Blacks are delivering—ah...but do not talk about it. Legendary producer Spike Lee, tried to bring awareness to this virus in his classic movie "School Daze" (1988).

Many national Black organizations attract many light-skinned Blacks based on fraudulent perceptions that lighter skin is more attractive. In addition, participation in these groups ensures lighter skin privilege and group continuity. This is a misconstrued position to adopt. And not one those organizations' leadership sanction, this author is sure, but it seems to be undoubtedly a part of those organizations culture. Views and acts such as these suggest many remain plantation-ized.

Sadly, the dominant population defines for the most part, Black's outlook on beauty. In particular, Blacks who deny their Blackness or modifying their African features for celebri-ty, fortune or career mobility in American society.

Moving past this self-imposed demarcation is critical. There cannot be any form of unity as some champion, when Black people remain divided based on skin. There can be no true unification when some Black people believe because they possess the former master's blood, they are superior and their darker brother and sister feel a sense of inferiority because they have none or not enough. The outcome of such a lofty aim might turn the corner on some little Black girl cogitating they are not beautiful. It may enhance the self-esteem of a boy who is referred to as "Blackie." Who knows they may grow up to become president of the United States.

> *"The Black skin is not a badge of shame, but rather a glorious symbol of national greatness."* —**Marcus Garvey**[24]

Demand for a race Discussion

Several of the brightest Black minds in academia posit a national dialogue on race is needed. They have appeared on talk shows advocating for this great American debate. Moreover, they argue Black people should engage in a conversation, which speaks to what Frederick Douglass claimed to be the *"Great sin and shame of America."*[25]

These enlightened academics assert a glorious outcome will be realized from this dialogue. Yet this is strange reasoning when the majority population has selective amnesia on the issues of slavery, racism and poverty. Most of white America still has a negative view of Black people, as previously mentioned and shun this type of dialogue.

Nor have Black Intellectuals, who advocate for this sit down made clear the benefit of this conversation. Although, dialogue, discussion and debate can bring remedy to open issues on many occasions as previously stated. This conversation framing needs further clarification. But, in lieu of the current legal decision in the Trayvon Martin case, perhaps dialogue is the only option. Nothing else seems to be working in this area of white desperation to retain power.

Many Blacks may welcome the opportunity to share reality with those of the white dominant population that deny or minimize the residue effects of institutionalized slavery and Jim Crow. As well, articulate how this society continues to benefit from nearly three hundred years of free labor— downgrading the atrocities, yet, displaying the prosperity received as a nation, but not sharing the wealth.

So, that being stated, dialogue regarding basic human rights, freedom and equality today in America, still remains surprisingly necessary. America, the supposed land of the free, where democracy reigns supreme has major racial issues, it always has. Most Black men know this first hand. America, some suggest is the most racially divided nation on the planet. History states, oppression, suppression and racism in the United States were and remains like no other.

Yet, some questions must be answered before this healing conversation is under taken. Which suggests a meaningful racial conversation is not possible in the near future.

Keeping in mind, with recent events (economic uncertainty), the country's interest has been diverted—Blacks and Whites alike. In particular, Black consciousness seems to be waning, and white attention has shifted to the Hispanic/Latino, LGBT and other movements.

Also, to argue freedom, human rights, and equality to the world, but not perfect it within your own borders, seems hypocritical. Is America duplicitous in its actions? Of course, this is proven daily.

From dialogue with the majority populace—what is hoped to be gained...calling white America hypocritical? This has already been done, and still done—frequently. What has not been said or not heard before? What is different from the arguments made by David Walker, Frederick Douglass, John Rock, Martin Delany, Martin Luther King Jr, Malcolm X, James Farmer, James Baldwin, Stokely [Kwame Ture], and Jesse, as well as countless others on freedom, equality and human rights, or simply put ones "Unalienable rights"?

Dialogue may commence at the kitchen table, however, national discussion must be drafted where substance is debated for meaningful results.

Additionally, Black America must be convinced of the relevancy to engage in dialogue. Despite Black consciousness waning, Blacks in general still do not see any benefit discussing with a society that has looked down, castigated and treated Black people sub-human for hundreds of years. Today Black people want jobs, housing and safe streets—not more talk from politicians, academics or spiritual leaders.

Furthermore, most intellectuals may not have given thought to how the masses think regarding this topic. Since they spend their careers in the ivory tower and only take up an issue when a well-publicized tragedy occurs. Maybe they conceptualize the elites and academics of the community only should take part, and speak for the Black masses in this forum. Perhaps just leave it to the modern *Talented Tenth* or possibly the *Very Intelligent Negros*. Let us just reinstitute the American Negro Academy and draw from that group. For sure, hold these discussions at an elite Ivy League institution.

Similarly, who speaks for the white population? Whom do the intellectuals propose, represent the majority white population in this great debate? The majority populace might not want to face the acts of their ancestral past. Some can and do argue that was then... let it go! Let us deal and live in the now! We elected a Black President twice; come on, let us get past this.... Let us move on!

Of course, this would be a form of avoidance or "White-nesia." But, really, who wants to discuss oppressing and suppressing people? Who wants to talk about owning another human being as property like a dog, a cow, or a horse, and using the property to breed and work all day in the hot sun? So the owner can feed his family and make profits. Who wants to talk about mating with what W.E.B. Du Bois would consider a *tertium quid;*[26] described more commonly as a clownish individual, and enslaving the offspring of the act. Then if need be, selling the offspring to enhance the master's fortune without hesitation.

Additionally, who wants to talk about ending slavery, and

then re-enslaving the same people with peonage and false criminal charges (convict leasing).[27] Moreover, debating centuries of murdering, manipulation, raping, repudiation of basic human rights and civil rights, unsanctioned medical experiments and saying it was God's will. Who wants to talk about dogs attacking a human being, just because he or she wanted to exercise their constitutional right to vote? Let alone, discuss political exploitation, constant poverty, second-rate educational opportunities, and substandard housing? But routinely claim everyone is entitled to equal opportunity under the law.

No one knows whether a national race discussion will ever take place. However, what is known—Black people do not talk willingly about their business. Allowing a stranger into the kitchen cabinet is not common practice.

This suggested dialogue, along with the government's theoretical abilities to repair centuries of mental mutilation and emotional castration, will require significant thought. Will this conversation provide shelter from the cold and the hot sun with running water, as well as put food on a table? Will the conversation get the same response President Obama got from conservatives and tea party members after he bequeathed to the world his race speech prior to his election as president or drawn their irk after his brief race comments after the Trayvon Martin verdict?

Moreover, will the dialogue turn the tide on the senseless

killings, landfill of self-abasement, or decrease the level of unemployment that blankets so many Black men's lives.

It is clear many questions remain unanswered. But, to have a fruitful dialogue, Black men must resolve the problems in their own homes before they invite a guest over for dinner and conversation. How is it possible to engage in conversation with society when Black men cannot even talk among themselves about the issues of the community? To forgo deliberation first among family, friends and neighbors—is irresponsible.

The Fear...You not Black

Many from past generations, often ask why do Blacks of this era do not talk among themselves. From the current picture, it can be deciphered—many Blacks cannot rationalize the struggle. They do not see covert racism or have experienced overt racism and discrimination as in the past. Furthermore, they are beneficiaries of the various movements, thus they conceive the struggle is over. Likewise, most have become ardent integrationist. Their focus is self-centered, as is the American way.

Equally, fear, can also be reasoned why most Black men do not discuss in-depth the lunacy that encapsulates many Black people lives, and other pressing community topics.

Fear drawn from the truth, regarding the Black community's complexity restricts conversation. This includes its positives attributes, shortcomings, and self-induced vices. Fear keeps Black men quiet, dreading no longer being identified as a part of the neighborhood that bore them. Loss of the so-called hood pass is frightening for those, who still believe they have one. Fear prevents engaging family members, friends and associates concerning attitudes, behavior and wrongs that plague the community daily. Blacks tend to believe they will no longer be viewed as Black, for those who consider being Black still means something.

Many Black people dread the label of elitist, or worse being considered a sell-out. They do not want to be viewed as the uppity Negro, who has forgotten where they or their parents/grandparents came from. The fear of being viewed in the same vein as William Hannibal Thomas, Clarence Thomas, a snitch, the police, coined a modern-day Uncle Tom or a neo-conservative Republican is unthinkable for some. Fear also prevents confronting racism and discrimination to keep a job or get a promotion.

Likewise, certain Black men are embarrassed about their history—about slavery. Others feel ashamed of their drug-dealing or incarcerated family member, their sister with multiple children by different daddies, high school dropout cousin and their own troubled child. In addition to, the community issues that tend to follow Black people wherever they go. This feeling of embarrassment negates conversation.

Conversely, not understanding the fear to engage in dialogue about the past, present and future hinders progress. It limits opportunities to shape views, share opinions and establish common ground. Thus, the challenge to the faith-based organizations, the Alphas, Kappas, Omegas, Sigmas, Iotas, Masons, Shriners, Elks, and barbershops in every Black community is to engage in conversations about the current Black experience.

Reviewing the past, envisioning the future and analyzing the continued impact of the enslaved mind might change the course for Black men in this society. These conversations might elevate thinking that frees them from mental shackles.

Yet hesitation persists...Why? When will Black men admit they do not like other Black men calling them Nigger or Nigga? Additionally, recognizing all Black men do not think alike. Nor do they adhere to the same belief system, politics, spiritual views and aspirations. At the same time, admitting internalized racism hurt and hinders. And like other groups of the general population, some Blacks will become affluent, and others may not be as fortunate.

When will one be able to convey their interests and thoughts without considering the pushback of some social group claiming Black people, with different opinions are not sensitive to the community (this is different from the Overcame Brothers and Black denial)?

Fear of personal attacks, vilification, and ostracizing by family, friends and the old neighborhood keeps those with a different view—silent. Not being Black enough (whatever that means), down for the cause, fear of being chased out of the barbershop, unwelcomed at the block party or family reunion are powerful motivators to remain quiet.

Thus, a common platform-like the liberation of the Black man's mind or support for higher Black learning and self-awareness might be unattainable.

The Black community is built on shared historical experiences. Dialogue will pull Black men closer together not apart. **Brothers... Pull UP!**

"Let us make the effort to be the best of ourselves."
—Marcus Garvey [28]

CHAPTER FIVE
Denial of Blackness
■ ■ ■ ■ ■ ■ ■ ■ ■

*"The evil of internal division is wrecking our existence as a people,
and if we do not seriously and quickly move in the direction of a
readjustment it simply means that our doom becomes imminently
conclusive"*—**Marcus Garvey**[29]

EVEN IN LIEU of current events, many Black men, still hesitate to commence dialogue, on this issue, although it weighs heavy on their mind. They seem to dread what others might say or think. Thus, they fail to initiate critical discourse with a sense of urgency. When Black men attempt to engage in conversation on this topic, it is normally in a jesting manner. If they say, something meant—no one will take it serious. So, they walk around this most crucial topic at the kitchen table, the barbershop, the Black church and fraternity meetings. Additionally, Black men jump around the subject at their middle and upper-middle income socials (Dinner Dances, Jazz Brunches, Boat Rides, Golf Outings, etc.) where they differentiate themselves from others less educated or fortunate.

In contrast, conversation the African American communities meet with trepidation take on a robust life making the rounds on conservative television and radio talk shows. The topic comes to life as the butt of old and new comedy show skits, garnering laughter from Black and White audiences alike. Many professors teach about the subject at colleges and universities nationwide, and students earn grades from test and assignments on—*the challenged Black male.*

Thoughts about Black men always stir reaction. Currently, because of the accomplishment by President Barack Obama, attention has been generated on certain types of Black men. The media follows success stories like Deval Patrick, *governor of Massachusetts*, Kenneth Chenault, *chairman & CEO of American Express,* Cory Booker, *US Senator, New Jersey* and Jay-Z, *entrepreneur and entertainer,* and others.

While, we should celebrate the success of these accomplished Black men, as society customarily focuses on the Black man's failures. The continued challenges and struggles of Black men in this society are always a topic. And due to lack of internal dialogue, discussion and debate in the Black communities, the majority population is allowed to highlight its concerns about the Black male; consequently, putting forth their own manifesto.

The inability to discuss, in earnest, this topic is cheating Black men and future generations of Black males. Robbing them of direction, role models and leadership; allowing some to continue down the path of ignorance, internal oppression and self-derogations. This must change... but how?

Perhaps, the death of *Trayvon Martin* and countless other unnamed victims whose names are just as vital, but do not make the headlines will help stimulate action. Maybe having a two-term Black president will motivate Black men to act.

A solider for unity, an activist for social change, or a Black scholar, the likes of, W.E.B. Du Bois, Chancellor Williams, Asa Hilliard and Molefi Asante are not the calling for everyone. Not all Blacks lived during the Civil Rights, Black Power, and Black Arts movement neither are they expected to relive it. However, they should acknowledge, respect and appreciate the outcomes from it. Afros, black shades and dashiki, these signs of self-expression are no longer in fashion. Every day the Black experience grows more diverse and the Black male with it. America can no longer deny his existence.

The Denial

Although society does not make attempts to deny the existence of Black men any longer (marginalize, yes—denial, no). Now certain Black men do the denying. And this denial appears to go deeper than the failure to take ownership of their role in the home or community. This denial manifests in the desire to separate, and be deemed by the majority population as different. This is nothing new, but it is alarming, as this frame of thinking grows more common.

Countless Black men spend significant energy divorcing themselves from the realities of the Black experience. While trying to reshape or redefine the majority's opinion of them as individuals. They do not wish to be included in the Black discussion. This position reminds one of *Black Skin-White Masks* by Frantz Fanon, who asserted the only destiny for Blacks, is to become white.[30]

This frame of thinking causes certain Black men to dissociate themselves from anything considered Black. Their unwillingness to be aligned with the Black masses and ill-suited stereotypes drives them into the arms of the descendants of their ancestors former transgressors for validation. Just as a slave once sought his master's approval or a son seeking approval from a father, these men in denial seek approval and acceptance from the majority population as the benchmark for success.

" The slave instinct has not yet departed from them. They believe they can only live or exist through the good graces of their masters."—**Marcus Garvey**[31]

Moreover, they take on new characteristics. Besides being anti-black, or a Rotary club and Lions club member, they become staunch Republicans, change religious denominations and friends—whatever will make them different.

Denial demands shelving Blackness to assimilate into a Eurocentric acceptable social order. Therefore, Black men in denial shun a Black concept of self to be a part of the right corporate office mix, right country club, right church and to live in the so-called right neighborhood. Those in denial are often found by their actions, yelling... see me; I am not like them; I am like you. My kid goes to school with your kid. I live in your neighborhood. I eat quiche too...I love it. I am not Black. I don't see color; I am just an American!

E. Franklin Frazier inferred some of these people exist as the *Black Bourgeoisie,* over fifty years ago. The modern actions of the *Overcame Brother* reaffirm their continued existence.

Without a doubt, many Black men live the dream (European-American Dream); this is the aim for most if you ascribe to Eurocentric normalcy or the American way. While true, at every turn one should seek to improve himself and the well-being of his family, but at what cost. Adopting the status quo, of individuality and capitalism could mean a person does so— regardless of whose neck they step on, whose back they whip, whose land they steal, or mother they rape (figuratively). However, not everything in the status quo is unacceptable (safety, comfort, nice neighborhoods, good schools, recreation and leisure, health benefits, material wealth and eating well).

Most men want a home, nice car and a good school system for their children, a well-paying job, and a safe environment in which to live. To achieve this station and status, most Black men embrace the value systems held by the dominant population. Some argue....Why would they not. Considerable evidence suggests that Black Americans are more American than most. Blacks have made profound contributions to building this nation as mentioned earlier.

Empirical data states Black men did not stand on white America's shoulders, but America undeniably stood on the Black man's back. And the design, which illuminates Black America, although, forced upon it—is a memento from their previous captors and transgressors—which includes language, religion, beliefs, and traditions. Thus, denial necessitates Black men to incorporate a modern day *House Negro ideology*—for some, this is the apogee of their existence.

> "The good slaves have not yet thrown off their shackles."
> —Marcus Garvey[32]

When you have no other frame of reference, mimicking the dominant population is normal. Black men have attempted to emulate the majority population for hundreds of years. This has been and still is the norm; except for a brief moment in time. After reconstruction, self-help manifested, followed by Marcus Garvey and the UNIA, but not until the Civil Rights and Black Power Movement, was there real change in Black identity. During the 1960s and 1970s, Black America adopted a new definition of self, which promoted an agenda centered on Blackness.

That is no longer the case—what happen? Instead, the majority of Black America is hook line and sinker pseudo European-American. Most Black people embrace and incorporate nearly everything from the white majority population. Even though, they are not afforded the same privileges (just waiting for the post-racial windfall). Black Americans are descendants of people, who have been captured, displaced, relocated, enslaved, and stripped. Now they are more like their captors, than their ancestors.

"Even if Negroes do successfully imitate the whites, nothing new has thereby been accomplished. You simply have a larger number of persons doing what others have been doing. The unusual gifts of the race have not thereby been developed, and an unwilling world, therefore continues to wonder that the Negro is good for."
—Carter G. Woodson[33]

The Denial is Egregious

Prior to 1865, more enthusiastically since the signing of the 13th Amendment of the United States Constitution, most Black men, have adopted a pseudo assimilation mindset. In the past because of force adaption—now, out of confused necessity—anything else would be deemed anti-social, radical, or white-hate by pseudo assimilated Blacks and the White majority.

But for Black men in denial, the desire to pseudo assimilate, drives them. Hence, they persist to emulate the majority culture, repudiating any other views or concepts.

And because of their apathy, they refute Black-awareness, as it serves no purpose in the world they subscribe to. Black

[66]

abnegation on this level should be alarming. For this mindset, leaves a Black man without a home, as he surfs between the white and Black worlds, never feeling at peace in either.

Regrettably, certain Black men's denial is so egregious that they have adopted a naivety as displayed by the character *Carlton* on the old *"Fresh Prince of Bel-Air"* television show (1990-1996). Their efforts and behavior are centered on proving they are a copacetic non-threatening Black man.

Denial blinds them to the reality that irrespective of their middle and upper-middle class stakes and beyond. As well, their home with a two-car garage and multiple college degrees—due to the pigmentation of their skin, they will never achieve the ultimate acceptance; at least not in the near future.

Thus, Black men who refuse to use their second sight are limited, as they solely see through a European lens, remaining blind to yesterday, confused today, and ignorant to the progressive possibilities for tomorrow in a changing society.

"It is a peculiar sensation, this double-consciousness, this sense of always looking at one's self through the eyes of others. One feels his two-ness - an American, a Negro; two souls, two thoughts, two unreconciled strivings; two warring ideals in one dark body, whose dogged strength alone keeps it from being torn asunder."
—W. E. B. Du Bois [34]

Consequently, for those in denial—their stark realization comes when the white police officer pulls them over. The police officer does not know, nor does he care about the top rank school or Ivy League education. The officer is not interested in the prestigious job title, upscale neighbor, membership at the local country club, nor the summer vacation home in Martha Vineyard. The driver fits the description or worst his perception of a likely suspect....BLACK!.... License, registration and insurance please....Step out of the car!

Reality also hits when passed over for a promotion deserved, or never seeming to get that pat of approval on the back. Moreover, discovering colleagues on the job are paid a few thousand dollars more doing the same work. Worst, the beloved child who is doled over living in the upscale neighborhood and attending the highly rated school wants to change his name from Leroy, Kenya or Jamal to *Josh or Jacob.* **Brothers...Pull up!**

"This modern house Negro loves his master. He wants to live near him. He'll pay three times as much as the house is worth just to live near his master, and then brag about "I'm the only Negro out here." *"I'm the only one on my job." "I'm the only one in this school." You're nothing but a house Negro. And if someone comes to you right now and says, "Let's separate," you say the same thing that the house Negro said on the plantation. "What you mean, separate? From America, this good white man? Where you going to get a better job than you get here?" I mean, this is what you say. "I ain't left nothing in Africa," that's what you say. Why, you left your mind in Africa." –Malcolm X* [35]

CHAPTER SIX
SOCIETAL PERCEPTIONS
■■■■■■■■■

"I will say then that I am not, nor ever have been in favor of bringing about in anyway the social and political equality of the white and black races – that I am not nor ever have been in favor of making voters or jurors of negroes, nor of qualifying them to hold office, nor to intermarry with white people; and I will say in addition to this that there is a physical difference between the white and black races which I believe will forever forbid the two races living together on terms of social and political equality. And inasmuch as they cannot so live, while they do remain together there must be the position of superior and inferior and I as much as any other man am in favor of having the superior position assigned to the white race. I say upon this occasion I do not perceive that because the white man is to have the superior position the negro should be denied everything." —**Abraham Lincoln**[36]

FOR CENTURIES, concocted perceptions of the Black male has generated an enhanced landscape of ethnocentrism and xenophobia here and aboard; perpetuating Black men with a negative skew—fostering belief systems that aggrandizes white superiority. The need to display Europeans and European-Americans as the standard-bearers of ancient and modern civilization has been a farce to excuse the atrocities implemented because of avariciousness.[37]

Thus, many in white America yesterday and in many regards today, attempt to maintain this negative construct of Black people, in particular, Black men. A stage has been constructed, better yet, a studio (America) where a live daily theatrical production (conquest, capitalism, slavery, racism, war, Black codes, jim crow, crime, convict leasing, civil rights, voting rights, affirmative action, drugs, prison, presidential elections, etc.) is performed, presenting a distorted narrative.

For over five hundred years, Black people have performed as ill-fitted supporting actors taking clues and direction from white leads. Whites write and produce the daily performance. They set the scenes and gather up all the actors (African slaves, slave-owners, overseers, drivers, white women, insurrectionist, uncle toms, abolitionist, soldiers, ku klux klan, lynch mobs, segregationist, activist, reformers, segregated buses, marchers, integrationist, radicals and transformist) creating a screenplay with an embellished narrative; rewriting history and prospering at the expense of the African. Whilst promoting white dominance as part of this societal development.

Blatant obfuscation of Black historical contributions to America and the world for centuries has been written out of the screenplay, making the play a top grossing production amongst white people. Even now, most educational systems fail to include Black American contributions or their experiences as a part of the historic and modern social fabric conversation. If introduced, it usually is by a progressive college or university, resulting from the struggle for liberation or a recent tragedy. On a rarity, a forward thinking school district where the conversation is brief and limited to the transatlantic slave trade, the civil rights movement, Martin Luther King, Jr., and now Barack Obama introduces the Black experience.

Because of the limited sharing of Black American experiences, most fail to realize, Europeans designed the historical construct, as it was necessary to justify slavery, as well as the theft of Africa's resources.

Before the stated quote above from Abraham Lincoln, another revered historical figures of this country, Thomas Jefferson highlighted the profound contradicting aspects of America's society then and now. Jefferson is credited with being the principal drafter of the *Declaration of Independence* and penning the words, "We hold these truths to be self-evident, that all men are created equal, that they are endowed by their Creator with certain unalienable rights, that among these are Life, Liberty and the pursuit of Happiness"(US Declaration of Independence, 1776). These words did not apply to Black men of course. Jefferson possessed an antithetical view regarding Blacks who slaved on his plantation.

Thomas Jefferson attitude was clear that Black people were inferior to whites in all regards. He espoused this disposition as he enriched his life on the backs of his Black slaves, while he carried forth a relationship with a minor deemed mere property. History told by others, romanticize this adult male and young female teenager slave sexual relationship. But under today's laws and social standards how might Mr. Jefferson be judged?

Thus, egalitarianism remains far from the America promoted and preached—irrespective of a Black president. Equality for all citizens, the aim on paper in the "Declaration of Independence" and "United States Constitution" is commendable. Yet, it goes unrealized. Nor was it ever intended for the African at the country's onset. Maybe one day, but as stated earlier, it is not present today. Visceral racism seems to be an ingrained characteristic of many in the dominant cultural hegemony as suggested by Irving Thalberg,[38] or a part of the fabric of America as inferred by the National Advisory Commission on Civil Disorders 1968. Which claimed, "Our Nation is Moving toward Two Societies, One Black, One White—Separate and Unequal" (Kerner Report, 1968). Contemporarily this society presents a picture of the have and the have not, with race and ethnicity remaining the dividing factors still.

Since Emancipation

Hence, one hundred and fifty years after the signing of the Emancipation Proclamation, many still perceive the Black

[72]

male as a belligerent, partying, singing, dancing, and now a basketball dunking, rapping, football running—modern Sambo. And that Black males are genetically predisposed to perform at a low level except in sports and entertainment.[39]

A significant part of the majority population seems to accept as the truth—society presents everyone an equal opportunity today to succeed, and certain Blacks are incapable of capitalizing on the opportunities. Asserting Black men, rather blame others for not achieving, then taking self-ownership.

Similarly, implying Blacks' boisterous nature, along with inadequate intellectual abilities, and buffoon behavior validates routine typecasting in movies. Thus, Black men are forced to play, for the most part, the cool coon, slick street thug, over aggressive police officer, not so-smart athlete—who needs saving by white folk, pimp, drug dealer, gang members or maladjusted fools, jokesters, historic Black figure and on occasion—the president.

Those are typical roles unless you are a limited few who achieved box office success such as, Denzel Washington, Will Smith, Forest Whitaker, Morgan Freeman, Don Cheadle, Tyler Perry and Laurence Fishburne.

Unfortunately, it is these stereotypes and demeaning misrepresentations, which contribute to an imbalance within the justice system. Routinely, Black men are given lengthier prison sentences than their white counterparts for the same offense. This injustice is well documented and known within the Black community. However, those who prosecute the cases, and handle the sentencing readily deny it.

A recommendation is made for anyone interested, to observe a courtroom in a city or town where there is a Black and white population; the injustice will frighten you. It makes one wonder if there are two legal systems: one for Blacks and one for whites. This might be shocking to the *Overcame Brothers...* so caution should be taken. At present, the practice of random stopping *"Stop and Frisk"* Black and Brown men, in major cities like New York under the disguise of putting into effect preventive measures to combat crime adds to the racism debate.

Perceptions appear to serve as the motivation for some police to shoot first and ask questions later (Sean Bell, Amadou Diallo to name two of many). Similar perceptions drove the government in the past to create laws, which distinguished between penalties on those drugs utilized by lower socioeconomic groups of people, and the drugs of choice of the affluent.

"When the Negroes were freed and the whole South was convinced of the impossibility of free Negro labor, the first and almost universal device was to use the courts as a means of re-enslaving the blacks. It was not then a question of crime, but rather one of color, that settled a man's conviction on almost any charge. Thus Negroes came to look upon courts as instruments of injustice and oppression, and upon those convicted in them as martyrs and victims." **—W.E.B. Du Bois** [40]

Likewise, aspersions casted by many in the majority con-trolled school boards against Black youth, who allegedly cause trouble, aids school districts to justify applying severe disci-plinary actions compared with white students for the same in-fractions.[41]

Do these perceptions surprise anyone? At one point, those who considered Black people less than human held tightly to these perceptions. They used them as reasons to segregate schools, restaurants, shops, etc. In addition, to beat, rape, mur-der, lynch, tar & feather, burn, drown, starve, breed and sell Blacks (*Men, Women and Children*) on a block...chained, na-ked or barely clothed. Not so long ago—just a little reminder for those Black men draped in **"Blacknesia."**

These disparaging views trigger white women to grab their children when a Black male comes near still in many are-as of the country. Many Black men can relate to this eye-opening experience...what an extremely sobering moment. These perceptions still drive white waiters or waitresses to presume Black people are going to stiff them on the tip.

Always in the room is the misplaced perception that Black male's lack intellect. Making it easier for little white boys to think their inherited birthright is to play quarterback; and for Black youth to play lesser cerebral positions. If the Black youth does play quarterback, it is attributable to him being a terrific athlete, not a serious thinker. Similarly, that white males, are predisposed to grow up to become lawyers, doctors, engineers and captains of industry. At the same time, Black males are to play the subordinate role. Those Black men, who do not play the subordinate role and do become a lawyer, doctor, engineer or captain of industry, are viewed as the exception. Dismissing the countless contributions, Black men make to society daily in all facets.

Regrettably, denigrating perceptions of Blacks have crept into other groups, as well. Ethnic groups, in particular, who sell Blacks liquor, fish sandwiches, dry cleaning and hair care products, seem to have adopted the majority populace views.

Even though income may be garnered from Black consumers, Black males, it seems are met with suspecting eyes. These groups appear to perceive Black men as inferior or criminals, similar to many within the majority populace. Also, their behavior suggests Black men have wasted opportunities to improve their position in America. Even Blacks from the mother continent and the Caribbean have fallen victim to these foolishness perceptions... Falling prey to divide and conquer, not realizing their conditioning, in many regards is worse than African Americans.

Not only, adults, but also minors call the character, integrity, and morals of Black males into question. Recently, at a treatment center a white male adolescent requested to be moved away from two Black male youth who were arguing. In a sharp tone, he stated he did not want their niggology (whatever that means) to affect him.

Thus, societal perceptions engrained in the fabric, formulated by concepts of supremacy drives many in the majority population view of the Black male contemporarily. Yet perceptions only live if mental disposition, behavior and attitudes keep them alive.

"This Charge of inferiority is an old dodge. It has been made available for oppression on many occasions."
—Frederick Douglass[42]

CHAPTER SEVEN
Acknowledge the Reality
■ ■ ■ ■ ■ ■ ■ ■ ■

My ignorance

Done things that require repentance,
Killed my brothers
Caused pain to mothers

Failed to stand as a man
Moved with no plan
Acted without thinking,
Mr. Charlie controls my movement without blinking

I 'am shook,
Don't like how I look!
Place no value in books,
Seen as a lowly crook by those who took

I hate
Most in America cannot relate
This hell, I must escape,
Abort the mission…. Stop! I refuse to self-annihilate
Clear my mind, cleanse my spirit, and free my body
I rebuke you… My ignorance

-- Baaki Tafiti, 2012[43]

NEGATIVE IMAGERY of Black men are forged into minds of the majority population during their earliest socialization by parents, teachers, community institutions, and the media—and the belief in white superiority sustains them as inferred by Roy Wilkins, Former Executive Director of the NAACP.[44]

Due to these belied assertions, the white majority maintains feelings of superiority—that they are the creators of all that is—*Good.* Conceptualizing, whites are the vanguard of humanity. Simultaneously, contriving Black males' sense of confusion, behavior and inferiority is a result of all that they are—*Bad.*

Unethical media and social institutions reinforce the multitude of deleterious metaphors, framing Blacks' ineptness daily. Questionable media portrayals speak volumes to why acts of foolishness; loudness and aggressiveness are the perceived standards for Black men, presenting an unprecedented challenge to overcome. Yet, the negative portrayal by the media is nothing new. They have always been used in America to depict Black men.

Some Blacks own the Perceptions

But, for some Blacks, as you are viewed, so you become. Hence, Black men who side with excuses and self-denigration—their reality stands true. For Black men who live by inferior thought, actions and excuses... their reality is the perceptions.

Thus, the struggle to be free from the stage show of distortions, where whites direct the play and too many Blacks play unsavory characters continues.

Amplification of so-called Black male deficiencies by the media, the justice systems, social service agencies and educational institutions has penetrated into the contemporary Black home. Wives, girlfriends, mothers and even children have brought into this inferior construct. But in their defense, if you were bombarded with adverse images of Black men, depicting them in a contemptuous manner, it would have a negative effect on any staunch support system. A husband, father, brother, son and provider portrayed as an aggressive, untrustworthy person who lacks self-control, intellectually weak, and full of excuses would be crippling to any man's family portrait.

This portrait has driven one Black author to suggest Black women should explore dating outside their race, possibly to improve their quality of life.[45]

Alternatively, other conversations hinge on how Black men display an abundance of enthusiasm discussing LeBron James and Kobe Bryant. But avoid dialogue on Black male high school dropout rates, or Black-on-Black crime, in particular, the murder rate. In addition, limited, or no conversation on community cures for poverty, baby-making machines, who do not provide for their children, HIV transmission to Black women, internalized racial oppression and gang violence. Why do dialogue at Black barbershops not center on these critical conversations, instead of focusing on what team won the game?

Thus, laughter of Black men supposed shortcomings will continue. Laughter, jokes and finger pointing about what is speculated as the Black man's incompetence to obtain employment during the best of times, and his lackadaisical pursuit of achievement during the worst of time. Opening the door further for conservative politicians, who make Blacks alleged disdain for education, perceived intellectual retardation and fixation on criminality talking points during elections. If Black men are not disturbed by this—they should be.

These perceptions suggest Black men provide nothing of value and just take from society, as Newt Gingrich and Rick Santorum posited during the 2012 Republican primaries. As they seem to see it, Black men cause havoc, and the majority white population continues to save the savage, providing illumination. Making it easier to digest falsehoods that Black men hold a proclivity to steal, kill, lie, cheat—not just to others—but more vehemently against other Black people. This is an arrogant position to hold...knee-deep in misinformation. Yet, because of societal circumstances, some reality to these assertions does exist.

The largest Black populated cities are stewed in flawed belief systems, pools of plight, held hostage by mis-education, unemployment and poverty; manifested by the continued residue of slavery and psychological imprisonment. This cannot be denied.

Unfortunately, some in the community seem to be waiting for the majority population to save them (White America). To provide a capital infusion of self-awareness, self-esteem and self-assertiveness (this is not going to happen). The quandary of issues afflicting many Black Americans need a remedy now, but it will not matriculate solely by the hands of the government or a care-given non-profit organization—Black efforts must be the catalyst.

Yet, while many Black men wait, people are dying around them. As they represent failure to break free of their slave residue. They cannot move forward in a society that is changing rapidly. Black people face becoming less relevant to the electorate for either party. The Latino, Asian and LGBT communities are moving upward, aggressively engaged in the political, economic and social fabric of this society. As these phenomena occur, many Blacks remain on the sideline scratching their heads, looking dumbfounded, clueless or afraid to engage in social change. Once, the champions of social change, now, many appear hapless, helpless and hopeless.

Rather than, engaging in some form of self-enhancement, community uplift, or civil discourse—they appear to be waiting for others to do what most should be doing. Trayvon Martin's death and many other innocents should be a repeated call to action for Black men to wake up their minds. The enemy in this fight is darker and greater than any weapon, drug, words, or systemic racism and discrimination. Continued unawareness by many Black American men has now become a malicious perpetrator, transgressor, suppressor and oppressor.

Thus, the hesitancy to tap out from distorted views, excuse rendering, victimization, self-abuse, and internal racial oppression ensures their reality will maintain the perceptions. Moreover, the failure to change the perception channel from negative to positive means being chained indefinitely to the dominant culture construct of alleged white superiority, privilege and purported Black inferiority.

Nearly thirty years ago in his work titled *"Community of Self" (1985),* Clinical Psychologist Dr. Na'im Akbar, suggested Blacks must develop their self-concept. He surmised knowledge of self, is the backdrop of mental emancipation. Thus, until mental emancipation occurs, regardless of who is in the White House or wins the NBA championship, Black men remain powerless and vulnerable to continuing the cycle of perceived inferiority.

Therefore, it is acknowledged that some perceptions are in line with the Black man's current state. **Brothers... Pull UP!**

"Nothing in all the world is more dangerous than sincere ignorance and conscientious stupidity"
–Martin Luther King, Jr. [46]

CHAPTER EIGHT
DESTROY THE PERCEPTIONS
■ ■ ■ ■ ■ ■ ■ ■ ■

LANGSTON HUGHES, after a troubling incident wrote *"Ne-groes, sweet and docile, meek, humble and kind: Beware the day they change their mind!"*[47]

It is quite clear... to destroy the multitude of perceptions used to depict Black men will require vast efforts. But efforts by Black men are only one part of the equation. Altering the majority population mental disposition is also necessary. This requires white America to make a concerted effort to transform their superiority attitudes toward others. Coming to grips with hundreds of years of complicit invasions, oppression, racism, discrimination and dehumanizing acts.

White society would need to rethink their belief systems and historical significance. Thereby, bringing into question white privilege and the construct of white dominance—this the majority of white America probably will not do without resistance. The attempt to change voting requirements in several key voting states in 2012 and recent acts by the conservative Supreme Court is evident. This is indicative of their historical response to change. The majority population seems to prefer absolution from the past and toleration of current acts of racism and discrimination.

Thus, white society's perceptions conversion, and the effectuation of America's mental emancipation may need to be left up to the continued demographic shift in the country. The political and social developments resulting from the shifting landscape are sure to shape views and opinion. As it is projected, the current majority will become a minority within several decades.

> "History is the long and tragic story of the fact that privileged groups seldom give up their privileges voluntarily."
> — Martin Luther King, Jr.[48]

Until then, Black men must continue to liberate their minds and master their passions. For centuries, Blacks had no say, more recently, with say—some continue to allow others to abridge their thought, movement and growth. In essence, they surrender their will, allowing methodical control over thinking and behavior. As a slave capitulated to his master after being whipped with the lash, as Black code laws sapped determination—some Black men seem to continue these traditions.

The conditioning is overwhelming

From the onset, it has been inferred, a European-American worldview influences the majority of Black minds. And because of this, most Black men allow others to drive their mental car, thereby, determining their direction as they continue to relinquish their judgment in this modern era. Thus, making it easier for perceptions to dedicate how Black children are raised and resources are spent. Moreover, how Blacks view and respond to one another.

Evidence of this continued control over Black thought is obvious when driving through a predominately-white community; because of their conditioning, Black men at once start to look for the police. Better yet, when a police car pulls up beside or behind, which is normally a short time thereafter, their level of anxiety elevates through the roof. The slave residue persists... the master is coming... the master is watching. So, Black men train their sons how to act when confronted by police, or how to behave in a department store... the master is watching... the master is coming.

Just the same, some Black men allow self-doubt to creep into their mind at the time of a job interview or employment evaluation; they start having *self-talk*. Convincing themselves, they are not going to be hired, or get a good job review because they are Black. While this may be valid, it speaks to heighten conditioning.

Equally, most Blacks are wired to view Black professionals as second tier to white professionals. So they spend their treasure with white professionals, under the guise their service is better. That white professionals received a superior education or possess a more extensive network. Yes, even today, this remains the thinking. Regardless, that the Black professional may have graduated from the same institution, received better grades, and higher scores on licensing exams.

This mental manipulation extends to something, as simple as going into a restaurant. Promoting Blacks to question what kind of service they will receive. Further, wondering if the white patrons are looking at them. So, they pray their children behave. When Black consumers enter an upscale mall to shop, the moment they hit the door; due to the likeliness of stares and glares, they straighten up and put on their most uppity display.

The conditioning is overwhelming, challenging Blacks to go the extra mile or be exceptionally better for an opportunity and consideration. These phenomena incite Blacks not to realize their self-worth. If Blacks perceive themselves as inferior and whites as superior, then their mind and spirit take on that persona.

Misconstrued, as they may be, what actions can be taken to decimate these persistent perceptions? There is a lot to combat; many suggest Blacks are fighting an uphill battle. Some state a battle that cannot be won, unless white America deems it so. This may be true to a degree… especially, if one depends on white America to determine their path.

Once, no one envisioned Black men free from enslavement, nor possess the right to vote in this society. Naysayers or non-believers argued a Black man would never be President (most Blacks expressed the view of not in their lifetime). Yet America is unfolding another chapter, and Blacks must assert themselves energetically in the text.

By undertaking the challenge to destroy the perceptions, Black men must address the overwhelming data, which claim almost half of all Black men, do not graduate from high school in this country. Moreover, that prisons and jails overflow with Black men, removing them from the home, the voting process, the education system and employment rolls.

In the same respect, Black men must address the fact that single women head the majority of Black households (no disrespect intended to the outstanding Black women holding down the family). And that a significant number of Black children are born out of wedlock or committed partnerships. Furthermore, that many Black children have become residents in treatment homes, juvenile justice system, and affiliated with gangs (products of ignorance, poverty, limited guidance and family disruption).

Simultaneously, Black men must address the merciless media and political manipulators who use the social construct of race as a means to excite their base. Moreover, Black men must abate the enabling mindsets and acts within the community that co-sign on foolish behavior of some fellow Black men. This includes parents, girlfriends, friends, community activist for hire, and the all-powerful enabling social service agencies.

What to do

The crisis Black men are immersed in; some more than others, begins with the residue of slavery. Which is like the stink of a skunk after being sprayed, you have to work to get it off. Slave residue influences mental and behavioral actions of parents, grandparents, uncles, aunts, and siblings. It stifles the whole community, including politicians, business executives and spiritual leadership.

Failure to teach self-awareness, cultural prominence, education valuation, appropriate behavior and life skills at the earliest age, serve as primary reason several issues discussed continue to wreak havoc in Black American communities.

Initial caregivers, early support systems, spiritual guides, and mentors carry the majority of the blame. They are guilty of failing to inspire, direct and redirect members within the family and community that exhibit illogical thinking, questionable behavior, self-contempt and denial—feeding the perceptions of the majority, helping to keep falsehoods alive.

Change requires growth of self, *no longer* being calumniated, castigated, defamed and viewed through a microscope by an uncaring media, and *I told you so* majority is acceptable.

Until Blacks change this, little progress toward destroying negative perceptions will be made. Discussion will continue to take place, ranging from inadequacies as fathers, to serving as terrible role models to their children, in particular, sons.

Dialogue will endure perpetuating Black men as incompetent, exposing an increasing record of disrespect and mistreatment of Black women by some. Lending support to various causation arguments on the dysfunctionally of the Black family. So, not until clarity of thought is realized, blinders on eyes and cotton in ears are removed will Black men fully comprehend perceptions effect on them, as well as their children's self-esteem, self-confidence and self-efficacy.

Until then, some in the majority population will continue to speculate how Black women tolerate Black men's inability to provide for them. Even though, these speculations do not consider the racist or discriminatory landscape that does not afford Black men similar opportunities to engage society. As well, receive the same benefits of capitalism. Nor, does it factor in a social domain that hinders Black males from experiencing the fullness of manhood.

Therefore, to achieve, at the highest levels, Black men must embrace critical thinking. Critical Thinkers, understand that progress depends on becoming liberators of thought, modifiers of behavior and curators of regulation.

To destroy perceptions, Black men must implement a series of steps immediately:

Step (1) Accept Responsibility

To commence the destruction of perceptions, Black men must first take ownership of their actions. Acknowledging as men, they are responsible for their existence, and not until they take responsibility of their mental state can they effectuate growth. Thus, refusing misconceptions and false perceptions, which hinder self-actualization and fulfillment of their destiny as productive and purposeful people is required.

Recognizing a major step for Black men is modification of blaming their state on the system or government. Although, there is more than sufficient evidence to support the system's role in diseducation, mis-education, mis-orientation, racism, discrimination and maintenance of ignorance and poverty, as well as planting the seed for internalized racism. Again, blaming...does what? What will it impact—what has it done... especially as white America moves away from the Black issues.

Black men have to control and develop the space they occupy. Thus, informed judgment and accepting responsibility are crucial for *stability and sustainability*. Upon taken ownership of being responsible for self—moving forward can begin.

Step (2) Self-Definition

Destruction of perceptions is a magnanimous task; so, it is

essential, for Black men to shape properly their views of themselves. The understanding of why one sees oneself the way they do is vital. Self-analysis to determine what makes one tick and what drives a person is essential. Self-reflection and introspection helps answer the question, *who are you.* Then build on this discovery.

Being self-assured and confident as a man is compulsory. **Marcus Garvey** stated, *"If you have no confidence in self, you are twice defeated in the race of life."*[49] Hence, being *"Unashamedly Black"* with knowledge of Black historical experiences in America and the rest of the African Diaspora is imperative. Marcus Garvey also suggested," *A people without the knowledge of their past history, origin and culture is like a tree without roots."*[50] Awareness of self must be the buttress to engage universally.

The challenge for Black men is not to accept the picture others implanted in their psyche. A worldview modification is required, shedding the Eurocentric worldview as the only lens seen through. Black men must see the world with all players as relevant actors on stage, above all themselves. Resisting ignorance, as many groups of slaves resisted bondage is essential to self-definition.

Step (3) Reconditioning the Mind about your Space

At once, Black men must start unlearning ideology inconsistent with growth and an enhanced quality of life. Cleansing impurities that cause errors in thinking is mandatory. Reevaluation of how Black men see and process their local space—along with what they have been taught about their place in it is required. A transformation must occur, seeing Blackness as fundamental, as anything learned about another.

It is imperative for Black men to see Black people overall, but, particularity those in their space as significant. Moreover, Black men must reassess what is deemed acceptable behavior within the space (community). In their space, Black men, must be seen as positive, contributing and accomplished; equally, appreciating and respecting growth, success and life. Thus, elimination of irrational belief systems harmful to development, stabilization, and enhancing one's space is paramount.

Step (4) Education Valuation

An unmitigated commitment to education is fundamental. Education is the impetus for change and growth. Diseducation, once the law throughout the land, now seems to be a self-induced virus. Upon being freed, Blacks desired reuniting with family, acquiring land and an education. Formalized education and a marketable skill can afford an individual a more comfortable lifestyle.

Education is tied directly to social mobility in this country. A marketable skill has been beneficial to Black men, even during the wretched period of slavery. Thus, Black men, must become committed learners. Erudite is a quality that can be immensely useful. The most fervent pursuit for education must always be made.

Step (5) Family Valuation

Just as advantageous as the above—valuing of the family is likewise crucial. Some may suggest more so. No man can achieve fulfillment without the support and love of others. Thus, the family should be held in the highest regard— realizing as a collective force, positive things can be accomplished.

One of the tragedies of slavery was the tearing of families apart. Black men must continue to build their family up, never bringing shame or harm to the family. Simultaneously, they must treasure the essences of the people, who make up the community, as they are extended family. Once these sequences of self-healing are completed, Black men can move forward tackling further issues, which require changing thinking and behavior one day at a time.

Moving Forward

It is scary, to still say, three men can be standing in an office: one Black, one White and one Asian. Black mind's automatically assume the white or Asian man is the boss, owner, or in command (although this remains true in most cases). This concept of inferiority has been ingrained into Blacks' cognitive framework—since enslavement. Therefore, failure to reject the Black status quo (faulty belief systems, inferiority concept, internalized racial oppression, elitism and denial) is not an option.

In his still relevant work, the Mis-education of the Negro (1933) **Carter G. Woodson** suggested, *"If you can control a man's thinking, you don't have to worry about his actions. If you can determine what a man thinks you do not have worry about what he will do."*

So, it can be surmised, lack of knowledge concerning Black self-worth is a cause of nationwide mental encapsulation. Continued acceptance of half-truths consistently kills minds and bodies. This is the underpinning of poor judgment, which has fostered an environment of chaos and underdevelopment of the Black spirit, family and community in many cases.

Some Black men must admit even in their own homes, there are those who embrace self-imposed ignorance. This is the case with all cultures. Even so, as discussed earlier, it would be understating damage caused by Black men, who prey on their own people, commit acts of violence, practice internalized racism, and justify the acts. No longer can this be rationalized. Black men must stop engaging in the plantation "Strongest Buck" mentality.

Sadly, this country has been built on the tolling of Black ancestors and other minorities. Black people have been mistreated, defrauded and historically dehumanized to say the least. Injustices continue today in various formats, which massage the psychological damage inflicted from centuries of oppression and suppression. This is debated daily. However, as offered earlier, some Black men still operate as breeders and fighting cocks; remaining detached from the woman and children in their lives. And one of the results of this disconnect is hundreds of thousands of Black youth filled with hopelessness.

While, it is known, the majority of Black men do not subscribe to poor choices, elitism, Black denial or spurious behavior. However, the segments that do—change is necessary or their space will be even more complicated. Destruction of the litany of perceptions will not be easy. It took time to cement them into Blacks and whites psyche, and it will take time to remove.

One can conclude, the immediate opponent to change is self—this usually is the case when limited thinking and the refusal to open the door to liberation of thought. Negative perceptions need to be destroyed by deeds, vigorous actions, understanding and willingness to overcome adversity. Thereby, proving all perceptions false, contrasted against accomplishments of excelling in the home, school and workplace will allow Black men to control how their story is told.

Therefore, no longer bragging about negative events in

the neighborhood or boasting about being from the hardest city in a song makes the grade. Forgo, pronouncing to the world, Blacks are the best ballers, hustlers and athletes. Repudiation of those who engage in deleterious acts, before and after countless efforts to redirect them must be a staple. In the same vain, Blacks cannot accept substandard teachers, administrators, or politicians in the community.

Rather, focusing on intellectual growth, economic stability and self-definition is vital. Reaching back in time and bring forth the thirst and energy of the past. In so doing, championing scientist, doctors, engineers and artisans, as well as those who move the image of the Black man forward in a positive direction should be the renewed march song. Intellect must be displayed as W.E.B. Du Bois, so surely advocated. All the while developing skills, trades and capitalistic markets, which Booker T. Washington suggested is essential. Recognizing Blackness, and taking pride in your race as posited by Marcus Garvey, also, has to occur at a greater level.

The opportunity to reshape society's views of the Black male has never been more readily available. Black men occupy positions of power in all spheres, disciplines and industries more than at any point in the history of this country. The chance to reframe the thinking among the masses to see the Black man for who he truly is—cannot be wasted or squandered.

During this time of economic upheaval, Black men must shine, not for the satisfaction of others, but for themselves. They must rewrite the play, creating a different narrative, with them as leading performers and the entire Black cast being relevant and valued. Severing the cord from centuries of brainwashing is past due. This may be the greatest moment in the history of this society for Black men to tell their story correctly. Finally, carving out more than a niche in this country, knowing that America is their country as well, because they built it; therefore, they must claim their vested stake. **Brothers... Pull Up!**

"Intelligence rules the world, ignorance carries the Burden" —**MARCUS GARVEY** [51]

CHAPTER NINE
THE TRUTH
■■■■■■■■■

"My friends, we can never become elevated until we are true to ourselves"—**John Sweat Rock** [52]

BEFORE AND SINCE ITS FORMULATION as the United States of America, this society has despairingly portrayed men of African descent as negative energy—this is well established. The Trayvon Martin case and the 2012 election should remind those, who elect to image otherwise. Routine defaming of men of African descent and their humanity is as common as a 4th of July cookout. The worldview created by greed, and the need to justify actions of theft, manipulation and a quest to display pseudo superiority is well documented.

This false sense of superiority and desire for power has become even more obvious. The hope of keeping white privilege alive appears to be in desperation mode. Nevertheless, as alluded, with altering demographics and glimpses of progression (attitude, respect, racial and ethnic tolerance) there continues to be optimism about the future.

That being restated, the truth is African American men are quite the opposite of the negative metaphors planted in the minds of people near and far. Only a minuscule of African

American men adhere to these hideous slants, no different from any other racial or ethnic group. But, even a minuscule is far too many, when the majority population historically uses those actions to define the whole.

The reality is Black men are complex, unique, steadfast, fascinating, lively, brilliant and exceptional people. Black men, the reported paternal line of human existence are likened to the poem *Invicitus*.

Invicitus

Out of the night, that covers me,
Black as the Pit from pole to pole,
I thank whatever gods may be
For my unconquerable soul.

In the fell clutch of circumstance
I have not winced nor cried aloud.
Under the bludgeoning of chance
My head is bloody, but unbowed.

Beyond this place of wrath and tears
Looms but the Horror of the shade,
and yet the menace of the years
Finds, and shall find, me unafraid.

It matters not how strait the gate,
How charged with punishments the scroll.
I am the master of my fate:
I am the captain of my soul.

- William Ernest Henley 1875

This poem captures the essence of the Black man's experience in America. The background of the individual who drafted this work is unknown and not necessarily relevant as the work speaks for him. It appears; he understood the struggle of man and the need to maintain dignity—whether one is Black, White or other.

Most within Black America recognize Black men as intelligent, sincere, hardworking and creative individuals. The black community sees them as positive citizens standing by the precepts, which make this nation true. African American men, have fought and died during the wars of this land. And they continue to serve this country with honor and distinguished service. Without question, Black men toiled in the fields, cleared the land, and built the roads, as well as the cities to make this country celebrated. And by the millions, Black men accept the daily challenges of life in this society. They stand tall, despite centuries of atrocities and adversity, as they carve out a space for them and their families.

Black men are pillars in their communities. Day in-Day out, they roll up their sleeves and go about the task of making notable contributions to their church, mosque, places of employment, school and other institutions. Facing challenges unequaled by any other racial or ethnic group, they continue to move forward. Their resolve is unparalleled. And the ability to hold heads up high when all seems hopeless is a testimony to the strength inherited from their ancestors.

Black men fight the good fight every minute of the day. Sincerely, they are committed to their wife and passionate about their children. As well, they are stalwarts in their profession or vocation. Black men are role models; their sons mimic their behavior. Additionally, they hold a distinct place in the hearts of their daughters and mothers. They are sensitive, nurturing, caring and attentive men. Engaged in the political process, they are defenders of right and warriors against wrong. Education is valued, as students, teachers and parents. They understand education is a powerful tool and the gateway to a more fulfilling life.

Moreover, Black men coach little league soccer, swimming, track, basketball, football and baseball. As well, fill a void as surrogate fathers for many. In addition, they mentor youth and care for seniors. Black men have knowledge of self, and a vision for tomorrow. They hold many titles such as, husband, dad, brother, son, firefighter, police officer, judge, doctor, pastor, inventor, engineer, educator, scientist, imam, counselor, truck driver, mason and president among many others. Just like other men, Black men are beacons of dignity, morality and goodness; standing tall, when their son's fall— helping them up, instead of not being there as often suggested.

Black men experience sorrow, crying for the loss of loved ones—as they feel just like the next man. However, rebounding faster, as they know life must go on, and much work is yet to be done.

These outstanding men exemplify what most men desire to be, and so-called therapists, counselors and social workers say men should be. They bring about positive change in the community and uphold the true tenets of being a responsible citizen and they deserve a... **PUSH UP!**

"Internal problems of social advance must inevitably come— problems, of wages, of families and homes, of morals and the true valuing of the things of life; and all these and other inevitable problems of civilization the Negro must meet and solve largely for himself, by reason of his isolation"
—W.E.B. Du Bois [53]

CHAPTER TEN
25 Things Black Men need to Reassess
■ ■ ■ ■ ■ ■ ■ ■ ■

DUE TO THE URGENCY, for community and self-repair there are twenty-five things Black men must immediately reassess in order to improve their quality of life in this society.

1. **If you make excuses for your current situation, consistently blaming others for your inability to obtain and achieve, you have not taken ownership of your life... Pull UP!**

   Total elimination of excuses is necessary. No more, I grew up in a bad neighborhood; I did not have a father; my mother was an alcoholic or on drugs. My family did not have money.

   Yes, Black men have had it extraordinarily hard in this country. Yes, they get the raw end; they always have. Yes, racism and discrimination is always present.

   However, no one is listening to this argument any longer. So let us not make it! Society is changing; it is no longer just Black and White. It is Black, White, Brown, Yellow, Red and everything else. In fact, it has always been that way, but African Americans need to pay attention to the changing of the guard and figure out their space. Keep striving!

2. **If you do not have knowledge of self... Pull UP!**

   In order to embrace life, you have to gain knowledge of self; you have to understand the '*Why and What*' in your life. Why are you currently were you are, why you do... what you do?

   What are your likes, dislikes, political views, your culture, family history, spirituality beliefs, etc.

.

3. **If you are not consistently seeking to improve yourself in a positive manner... Pull UP!**

   Growth and success requires constant effort and forward movement. Get moving now!

4. **If you are failing to lead by example and provide a sense of wellness for your family... Pull UP!**

   The stability and well-being of your family should always be your first priority.

5. **If you have no value of community, or are not active in its growth and development... Pull UP!**

   Next to your immediate family, where you live and fellowship—its growth, stability and prosperity must be valued and sustained.

6. **If you have not taken full advantage of opportunities to educate yourself and obtain a skill or trade... Pull UP!**

   You must seize the moment to enhance your abilities to provide for you and your family. If you cannot bring anything to the table besides your body, you will not eat.

7. **If you have not graduated from High School, or obtained a G.E.D... Pull UP!**

   It is highly unlikely that you will get through the door without one, and today that is far from enough.

8. **If you cannot read, nor write, and are not making an effort to learn to do so... Pull UP!**

   It is highly unlikely you will be able to complete the application.

9. **If you fail to listen to the voice that provides you with moral direction... Pull UP!**

   There is a little voice that we hear when we need to be Mindful... listen to it.

10. **If you do not have a spiritual base and have not recognized that life is a blessing from the creator... Pull UP!**

It is our faith that carries us during struggle, as well as calm.

11. **If you are a father and you do not take care of your children, e.g. pay child support, spend time with your son(s) and daughter(s) modeling positive behavior... Pull UP!**

As a father, you have a responsibility to be in your child's life to protect, provide financial, emotional support and stability. For your son, he needs you in his life to teach him how to be a man.

12. **If you Steal, Cheat, Sell Drugs, Rape, Rob, Shoot or other known criminal acts... Pull UP!**

Stop it now, it is wrong; it is immoral. Real men do not do these things.

13. **If you abuse physically, mentally or emotionally your wife, partner, or girlfriend... Pull UP!**

Are you serious, Coward!... Punk! Get it together!

14. **If you consider or call a woman a Bitch... Pull UP!**

Would you like someone to refer to your mother, grandmother, sister or daughter(s), as such, so do not do it!

15. **If you use the word Nigga, Niggard, or Nigger in any conversation... Pull UP!**

Anyway said, it is the most terrible word, stop it! Improve your vocabulary.

16. **If you consider yourself a Nigga, a Pimp, a Thug, a Gangster... Pull UP!**

So as you think, so will you act, so will society perceive you.

17. **If you embrace violence, and expose your children to it... Pull UP!**

Acts of violence destroy our communities. It is learned behaveior... Stop it now... Do not pass go!

18. **If you abuse your children... Pull UP!**

You must nurture and protect our future not destroy them.

19. **If you engage in internalized racism, Black denial, elitism or snobbery... Pull UP!**

Stop the foolishness; get a reality check and find yourself, you need to modify your views!

20. **If you use drugs or drink alcohol excessively, and are not in treatment... Pull UP!**

You must take the first step to help yourself... get help now!

21. **If you are consistently in and out of jail or prison... Pull UP!**

Pause; rethink your life goals and aspiration now.

22. **If you do not think critically about life and everything around you... Pull UP!**

Fulfillment of life is thought out; it is analyzed and planned. It requires strategy.

23. **If you live your life in the past, and consistently talk about yesterday... Pull UP!**

Yesterday was yesterday, you must never forget the past; you must learn from it. You cannot live in it... Push on!

24. **If you blame the white man for everything wrong in your life... Pull UP!**

You cannot let the past keep you encapsulated. Become engaged in your own direction, but never forget the conditions, which your ancestors and community have endured. You can not indict the whole for the acts of some. However, never put yourself in a position where you portray the role of an inferior human being.

25. If you do not vote—and not take it seriously… Pull UP!

Voting is essential; moreover, a responsibility of citizenship. It behooves all, who can, to do so. Your voice may not be heard, if you do not vote. Your vote is valued and needed.

"The power of the ballot we need in sheer self-defense,—else what shall save us from a second slavery" —**W.E.B. Du Bois** [54]

END NOTES

Chapter One
[1] Claude McKay, (1921) excerpt of poem "America"
[2] W.E.B. Du Bois (1903) *The Souls of Black Folks,* p.13

Chapter Two
[3] Langston Hughes (1959) excerpt from I Too Sing America, *Selected Poems of Langston Hughes.* p.275
[4] Carter G. Woodson (1933) *The Mis-Education of the Negro*, p.2
[5] http://surveys.ap.org/Published in Huff Post Black Voices October 27, 2012
[6] Carter G. Woodson (1933) *The Mis-Education of the Negro* p.44
[7] Na'im Akbar (1996) *Breaking The Chains of Psychological Slavery*
[8] Joy Degruy Leary (2005) *Post Traumatic Slave Syndrome*: America's Legacy of Enduring Injury and Healing
[9] Martin Luther King, Jr. A Testament of Hope: The Essential Writings and Speeches of Martin Luther King Jr., p.246
[10] W.E.B. Du Bois (1903) T*he Souls of Black Folk*, p. 45
[11] T. Anderson & J. Stewart (2007) Introduction to African American Studies ,pp. 129-136
[12] US Bureau of Justice Statistics (2011) Retrieved from http://www.bjs.gov/content/pub/pdf/p11.pdf).
[13] US Census Bureau (2010). Retrieved from http://www.census.gov/population/race/data/ppl-ba10.html
[14] Malcolm X, Retrieved on May 2013 from: http://malcolmx.com/about/quotes_articles.html

Chapter Three
[15] Black Voices, retrieved from http://surveys.ap.org/Published in Huff Post Black Voices October 27, 2012
[16] Manning Marable (2009) *Let Nobody Turn Us Around*, p.91
[17] Raymond Wolters (2003) Du Bois and his Rivals, p.90

Chapter Four
[18] James W. Johnson (1912) Autobiography *of an Ex-Color Man*, p.72
[19] P .L. Gay (1999) *Slavery as a sexual atrocity,* pp. 5-10
[20] W.E.B. Du Bois (1903) *The Souls of Black Folk*, p. 137
[21] Hine, Hine & Harrold (2010) *African Americans A Concise History* 3rd edition, p. 328
[22] Alexander Crummell (1883) *The Black Woman of the South*: Her

neglects and Her Needs, New York: Dover Publications, Inc.

[23] T. Anderson & J. Stewart (2007) Introduction to African American Studies ,pp. 173-193

[24] Marcus Garvey, retrieved on March 2013 from: http://africanamericanquotes.org/marcus-garvey.html

[25] Frederick Douglas (1852) Great Speeches by African Americans, Dover Publications, Inc. *What, To The Slave, is The Fourth of July?* pp.13-34

[26] W.E.B. Du Bois (1903) *The Souls of Black Folk*, p.122

[27] Douglas A. Blackmon (2008) *Slavery by Another Name*, p.83

[28] Manning Marable (2009) *Let Nobody Turn Us Around*: An Appeal to the Conscience of the Black Race to See Itself p.249

Chapter Five

[29] Manning Marable (2009) *Let Nobody Turn Us Around*: An Appeal to the Conscience of the Black Race to See Itself p.249

[30] Frantz Fanon (1961) *Black Skin, White Masks*, introduction p.9

[31] Manning Marable (2009) *Let Nobody Turn Us Around*: An Appeal to the Conscience of the Black Race to See Itself p.249

[32] Ibid

[33] Carter G. Woodson (1933) *The Mis-Education of the Negro,* p.26

[34] W.E.B Du Bois (1903) *The Souls of Black Folk*, p.45

[35] Malcolm X (1963) *"Message to the Grass Roots."* Northern Negro Grass Roots Leadership Conference. King Solomon Baptist Church

Chapter Six

[36] Michael P. Johnson (2001) *Abraham Lincoln, Slavery, and the Civil War*, p.73

[37] David Walker (1829) *David Walker's Appeal*

[38] Irving Thalberg, (1972) *Visceral Racism*, "Monist 56: 43-63.

[39] J.P. Gump (2010) *Reality matters:* The shadow of trauma on African American subjectivity

[40] W.E.B. Du Bois (1903). *The Souls of Black Folk*, p.201

[41] Chicago Tribune, Joel Hood , Study: Discipline harsher on African-American students in Chicago 3/06/212

[42] Manning Marable (2009) *Let Nobody Turn Us Around*:" What the Black Man Wants," Frederick Douglass, 1865 p. 126

Chapter Seven

[43] Baaki Tafiti (2012) *Poems by Baaki*

[44] Manning Marable (2009) *Let Nobody Turn Us Around:* Roy Wilkins

and the NAACP, p.363

[45] Karyn Langhorne Folan (2010) *Don't Bring Home a White Boy:*

[46] Martin Luther King, Jr (1963) *Strength to Love*, p.46 First Fortress Press

Chapter Eight

[47] Langston Hughes (1959) excerpt *"Warning"* from *Selected Poems of Langston Hughes,* p.167

[48] Martin Luther King, Jr. (1963) *Letter from the Birmingham Jail, April 16 1963*

[49] Marcus Garvey, retrieved March 2013 from: http://consciouspen.blogspot.com/2011/08/top-ten-sayings-and-quotes-by-marcus.html

[50] Ibid

[51] Marcus Garvey, retrieved March 2013 from: http://consciouspen.blogspot.com/2012/08/black-moses-seh-more-quotes-from-marcus.html.

Chapter Nine

[52] Manning Marable (2009) *Let Nobody Turn Us Around*: J.S. Rock, When ever The Colored Man is Elevated, p.107

[53] W.E.B Du Bois (1903) *The Souls of Black Folks*, p.137-138

Chapter Ten

[54] Ibid p.14

Bibliography

Akbar, N. (1985). The *Community of Self*. Tallahassee, FL: Mind Productions & Associates.

Akbar, N. (1996). *Breaking the chains of psychological slavery*.
Tallahassee, FL: Mind Productions & Associates.

Alexander, M. (2010). *The New Jim Crow*: Mass Incarceration in the
Age of Colorblindness, New York: The New Press.

Asante, M. (1980). *Afrocentricity: The Theory of Social Change*, New York:
Amulefi Publishing Company.

Blassingame, J. (1979). *The Slave Community*, New York: Oxford
University Press.

Blackmon, A. D. (2008). *Slavery by Another Name*: The Re-Enslavement
of Blacks Americans from the Civil War to World War II, New
York: Doubleday Broadway Publishing Group.

Bynum, M., Burton, E., & Best, C. (2007). Racism experiences and psychological functioning in African American college freshmen: Is racial
socialization a buffer?. *Cultural Diversity And Ethnic Minority Psychology, 13*(1), 64-71.

Clark, B. K. and Clark, P. M. (1947). *"Racial identification and preference
among negro children."* In E. L. Hartley (Ed.) Readings in Social
Psychology. New York: Holt, Reinhart, and Winston.

Chicago Tribune, http://articles.chicagotribune.com/2012-03-06/news/ct-
met-cps-civil-rights-report-0306-0120306_1_latino-students-
student-discipline-white-students.

Daley, J. (2006). *Great Speeches by African Americans:* Frederick Douglass,
Sojourner Truth, Dr. Martin Luther King, Jr. Barack Obama, and
Others, Mineola, New York: Dover Publications, Inc.

[112]

Du Bois, W.E.B. (1899). *The Philadelphia Negro: A Social Study.* Philadelphia: University of Pennsylvania. pp. 520. ISBN 978-1-163-25083-9.

Du Bois, W.E.B. (1903). *The Souls of Black Folk.* New York: New American Library.

Evans, A. B., Copping, K. E., Rowley, S. J., & Kurtz-Costes, B. (2011). Academic *self-concept in black adolescents*: Do race and gender stereotypes matter?. Self And Identity, 10(2), 263-277.

Fanon, F. (1961). *Black Skin, White Masks.* New York: Grove Press.

Franklin, E. (1962). *Black Bourgeoisie.* New York: Collier Books.

Fuller-Rowell, T. E., Burrow, A. L., & Ong, A. D. (2011). Changes in racial identity among African American college students following the election of Barack Obama. Developmental Psychology, 47(6), 1608-1618.

Gay, P. L. (1999). Slavery as a sexual atrocity. *Sexual Addiction & Compulsivity, 6*(1), 5-10.

Gump, J. P. (2010). Reality matters: The shadow of trauma on African American subjectivity. *Psychoanalytic Psychology, 27*(1), 42-54.

Harris-Britt, A., Valrie, C. R., Kurtz-Costes, B., & Rowley, S. J. (2007). Perceived racial discrimination and self-esteem in African American youth: Racial socialization as a protective factor. *Journal Of Research On Adolescence, 17*(4), 669-682.

Hine, C. D., Hine, C. W., & Harrold, S. (2010). *African Americans A Concise History: (3rd. Edition):* Upper Saddle River, NJ: Pearson Education Inc.

Hughes, L. (1959). Selected poems of Langston Hughes.

Johnson, W. J. (1912). *The Autobiography of an Ex-Color Man,* New York: Dover Publications, Inc.

Johnson, P. M. (2001). *Abraham Lincoln, Slavery and the Civil War: Selected Writing and Speeches:* Boston: Bedford/St. Martin's.

Jones, J. (1981). *Bad Blood: The Tuskegee Syphilis Experiment.* New York: Free Press.

Kerner Commission. (1968). Report of the National Advisory Commission on Civil Disorders, Washington: U.S. Government Printing Office.

Leary, D. J. (2005). *Post Traumatic Slave Syndrome*: America's Legacy of Enduring Injury and Healing; Portland: Uptone Press.

Marable, M. & Mullings, L. (2009). *Let nobody turn us around*: An African American anthology 2nd edition. Lanham, Maryland: Rowman Littlefield Publishers, Inc.

Muhammad, G. K. (2010). *The Condemnation of Blackness*: Race, Crime and the Making of Modern Urban America, Cambridge: Harvard University Press.

Pierre, M. R., & Mahalik, J. R. (2005). Examining african self-consciousness and black racial identity as predictors of black men's psychological well-being. Cultural Diversity and Ethnic Minority Psychology, 11(1), 28-40. doi:10.1037/1099-9809.11.1.28

Stewart, S. & Anderson., T. (2007). Introduction to African American Studies Transdisciplinary Approaches and Implications.

Thalberg, I. (1972). *Visceral Racism*. Monist 56 (1):43-63.

US Bureau of Justice Statistics. (2011). Retrieved from http://www.bjs.gov/content/pub/pdf/p11.pdf.

Woodson, G. C. (1933). The *Mis-education of the Negro.* Washington DC: Associated Publishers.